Holy Echoes

with God

Peggy Priest

Holy Echoes with God

Trilogy Christian Publishers, a Wholly Owned Subsidary of the Trinity Broadcasting Network

2442 Michelle Drive Tustin, CA 92780

Manufactured in the United States of America

10 9 8 7 6 5 4 3 2 1

Library of Congress Cataloging-in-Publication Data is available.

ISBN: 978-1-63769-900-3

E-ISBN: 978-1-63769-901-0

Cover design and illustration by: Anthony Caruso

To the glory of the Lord Jesus Christ,

and lovingly dedicated to my husband Carl...

Because he always believed in me,

even when I did not believe in myself.

Darren & Rosemarie,
I pray these stories are a blessing to you both :) Love You Guys!

Peggy Prust

JOSHUA 1:9

Preface

Have you ever asked for God to speak to you directly? I know I have. "Send me a fax, Lord!" I used to shout out. I know, that dates me, but you understand the concept. What I have found out over the years is that He does speak to me through the still, small voice in my heart, and what someone once described as "Holy Echoes."

This book is for someone out there who needs to hear these words and have faith that He is speaking to you. Sometimes He does speak to us directly, but often it is through the still, small voice during our everyday activities.

A smart person once told me that if you hear the same thing over and over through different venues, you are hearing "Holy Echoes" from God, trying to tell you something important.

I believe that "God stories" are when He speaks to you through events or daily, mundane tasks that seem unimportant. What I have learned over the years is that nothing is unimportant to God, and that He can use everything around you to teach a lesson.

The enemy wanted to destroy me and my family, but God intervened. We are all His testimony of what God can do to restore what the locusts have eaten (Joel 2:25). I could end the story here: but God intervened. That is such a powerful statement. However, you would miss out on all the fun stories that have brought me here today.

God has been so faithful to me through all my trials and

troubles. This book is my small offering to Him, giving back just a meager portion of what He has brought into my life. Jesus has shown me over the years that I need to yield to His will over many things. I pray that through this book, I will learn more about yielding to His perfect will daily in my life.

God's blessings in my life are here in a series of short stories, and I wanted to share them with you. I have also realized that the closer I get to God through His Word, the more I hear His voice and the lessons. Some people hide their stories in fear of what others might think. Others horde theirs for selfish reasons. I wanted to share these small snippets of my moments with God so that you can possibly see Him in your daily walk. I am just one "beggar" telling another where to find food. I also could not do this without His help, and my loving family's and close friends' support.

This book has been a lifelong project, as God has woven my life together through numerous trials and joys. My prayer is that through reading this book, one person can experience His peace—or that they hit the "aha" moment, realizing that He is often speaking to them as well. Then, I will consider it a success. The stories are short on purpose, to give you options. The cool thing about this book is that you can read it from cover to cover, or instead choose a chapter here and there. Either way, you won't miss the nuggets that God has shared with me each time you pick it up.

May God bless you as you continue your journey on this

small blue planet. As Paul the apostle said in 2 Timothy 4:7-8: "I have kept the faith. Now there is in store for me the crown of righteousness, which the Lord, the righteous Judge, will award to me on that day—and not only to me, but also to all who have longed for his appearing."

Praise You, Lord!

Peggy Anne Priest

Introduction

I should start with who I am and why you might want to read this book. I want to begin by stating that I am a flawed human being, but also a child of the King. Because of His infamous grace and mercy, I am here. If I had written just about myself, this would be a sad story of pain and reliance on my own strength. The beauty of these stories is that He has taken what could have been a train wreck and has slowly restored me into what He created. The stories here are a woven collection of what God can do with a willing soul and of how He speaks to me. "Holy Echoes," as I call them.

There is a Japanese term called *kintsukuroi* which, in layman's terms, means "golden repair." You may have heard this before, but if not, let me give you a quick explanation. *Kintsukuroi*, also known as *kintsugi*, is the art of repairing broken pottery through adding powdered gold infused with a lacquer dust. So, instead of throwing it away, it is "glued together," so to speak, with gold dust. The gold dust placed into the cracks highlights the repair as a symbol of its beauty. The philosophy is that it treats breakage and repair as part of the history of the pot, rather than something to hide. It shares the story of the object.

My life is akin to a *kintsukuroi* pot. I have felt very anxious about sharing what I have been through in life. I have often felt uneasy because I did not want others to judge me—or worse, to feel pity. I hate both. What God has shown me over the years is that my story, brokenness and all, is part of my history and what He has done through my weakness. I need to show my scars, and the gold He has used to mend my shortcomings, and to share with others that we are not alone in this journey. It is a lifelong journey that I will never complete until I am no longer here in this temporary home.

I grew up a child of the military. We moved every two to four years from base to base, until I was fifteen and my parents divorced. I grew up on military bases, and with each move I learned at a young age to plant roots closer to the surface, because you will need to move them sooner rather than later.

As you are probably starting to see, I did not know God as my Savior until I was an adult. I will share more of that later. I know; please, be patient with me. So many stories here.

I was a child of abuse and judged myself a terrible person because these things were happening to me. I cried myself to sleep many nights, praying that God would intervene and take my life.

In my deepest pain, I began the search for truth—the search for God. I remembered seeing that peace in others when we went to church on Christmas and Easter, and I wanted what they had. Maybe if I had that peace, my life would turn around, and I would not be the bad person I judged myself to be. I did not understand anything about His character of mercy and grace. I only understood God as the one I needed to clean up my act for first, and then come to Him. My self-image was so poor by that point that I felt insecure about my outer appearance and my inner capabilities. I wanted to look and act like a "good person" before I approached God.

That was a lie from Satan, because Jesus accepts us where we are, and then begins the process of healing and restoring us to Him. Saved by grace, not works (Romans 3:23-24). If I had known that grace could have saved me, I would have stopped my search instantly. However, since no one was there to tell me at the time, I continued in my own strength. God had birthed within me the desire to really know Him, but I had to go through more trials in my own strength before I would be ready to let go.

As I grew older, I became sidetracked by the world and taking control of my life. It was easier to press forward and not ask for directions. My philosophy, though distorted, was to do the opposite of what I grew up with. I am very grateful for God's patience in my life.

My family was dysfunctional at best. I knew I was loved, but often that love came with strings attached. When I left home, I decided to do things my way. A bad attempt at a Frank Sinatra song. I did not like the example my family had for marriage. I decided to not get married. I judged that I could raise children in my own strength. After three children and failed relationships, I realized I was spiraling. Raising kids, you realize you do not know as much as you thought you did before you started. I thought I could just "wing it," so to speak. As you can probably guess, it did not work out well for me.

I judged that I was not a good person or a good mother. I decided I needed to "fix" everything and get married. God knew that I needed more. The marriage was difficult at best and pushed me back to seeking Him once again.

That became my breaking point and brought me to the edge of the cliff. I needed to make a choice. Was I going to move forward in my own strength, or move once again to seek His instead? That brings us to this point. These stories are a compilation of what God can do with a lost soul and how He spoke to me along the way. My wish is that if these small stories give you hope or encouragement, you would please use those feelings and pay it forward to others around you.

Genesis 50:20, "You intended to harm me, but God intended it for good to accomplish what is now being done, the saving of many lives."

Joel 2:25, "I will repay you for the years the locusts have eaten—the great locust and the young locust, the other locusts and the locust swarm—my great army that I sent among you."

https://en.wikipedia.org/wiki/Kintsugi

Contents

Contents

Awakenings

Testimony

Sitting in my kitchen many years ago, I had no idea that my life was about to change so drastically. It was a crisp fall day. One where the sun dances between the clouds and shares its warmth with the fortunate one who can keep up with the music. The leaves were drifting along the yards gracefully, as if they alone held the secret to the song. Fall had arrived, and winter was quickly approaching. I admired the dance from my window, but I never left my chair to step out and join the music. Inside, I knew this dance was only a sign of change, and I likened change to visiting the dentist: necessary, but too painful for my taste. It was probably just as well that I was not aware of the changes which were about to take place on that cool autumn day.

You see, on that fall day, I accepted Christ as my Savior. This decision changed every part of my existence. It was not like some conversions, where the person is instantly different. There were no fireworks, no fanfare, no immediate joy. My conversion was more gradual, like that crisp fall day. It was there. It was happening. It was unstoppable.

The woman who prayed with me had listened as I talked about my bitter feelings toward my childhood and then my current problems in my new marriage. She offered to listen and to pray with me. Her first question after listening to me caught me off guard. She wanted to know if I had accepted Jesus into my heart. It seemed so simple, yet so profound.

I had been searching for the answers for many years. Was this the answer I was looking for? I had attended church and cried out to God so many times in my childhood. We had attended church on Christmas and Easter growing up. What I did not realize was that He did hear me.

He sent people to me over the years. Holy Echoes... One moment in life I reached out to a counselor at school, and she had a pamphlet on the table in the waiting room. I can still see that pamphlet. It shared a small story about how Jesus loves everyone, and even the drug addicts and others who had strayed from Him. I thought, in my twelve-year-old mind, *If He can love them, there might be hope for me.* What I did not realize is that the counselor was pressing her luck by placing these in a government school on base. She has no idea how it impacted me. Another "Echo" was when I was invited to church by my father's boss. I would sit in church and cry, feeling so unworthy. I had no idea that He was there with me, each step along the way.

I finally understood that God had been with me all my life, and that He wanted me to reach out to Him personally. I thought that this was amazing—that the God of the universe wanted to be with me! What I didn't realize is that once God has touched your life... you begin to change.

The prayers that followed were simple, yet they seemed to flow into my heart for the first time. I was ready. I repeated the prayer with the woman who led me to Christ. I did not feel any different right away.

I had never quite grasped this concept of change until it began to happen to me. I've always had an energetic spirit akin to a beaver in springtime, working hard all day. I put all my energy into my work. I scheduled everything around me and did not leave much time for myself. I scheduled daily, monthly, and life goals. If I could have, I would have scheduled when to go to the bathroom. I soon learned that God did not go by my schedule. I spent many tiresome hours wrestling with God over my unchanging spirit, until I realized, as Jacob did, that God does not change. Jacob wrestled with God to get his own way. I wrestled with God for the same reason. I believed I was going to win, as Jacob did.

What I was really wrestling with was letting go and trusting God with my life. Growing up with uncertainty and abuse, I had hardened my heart to trusting anyone. Trusting a God I couldn't see as a new believer was very difficult for me. There is a scripture that discusses how much our Father in heaven loves us, which is akin to our father on earth. Matthew 7:9 says, "Which of you, if your son asks for bread, will give him a stone?" Because my earthly version of my heavenly Father was tainted, I could not fully grasp that verse.

The Lord has been patient with my childish, unbending behavior toward change. I am not going to say it happened overnight. I am not even going to say I am completely flexible to change today. It is a daily battle that I can fight, knowing that He is by my side. Each day I learn to trust Him more, as He has never failed me since that first moment when I asked Him into my heart.

As I write this today, I see the yellow leaves falling from the trees, doing their familiar dance of autumn outside my window. The music of fall does not seem as scary as I remember. I think I will step out and join the music today; after all, change really is in the hands of our Lord. Step outside with me today and drink in His glorious creation!

Luke 15:4-7

"Suppose one of you has a hundred sheep and loses one of them. Doesn't he leave the ninety-nine in the open country and go after the lost sheep until he finds it? And when he finds it, he joyfully puts it on his shoulders and goes home. Then he calls his friends and neighbors together and says, 'Rejoice with me; I have found my lost sheep.' I tell you that in the same way there will be more rejoicing in heaven over one sinner who repents than over ninety-nine righteous persons who do not need to repent."

Baby Steps of Change

Each day after accepting Christ, I found myself drawn to know more of Him. I dove headfirst into the Bible. I made a personal commitment to study the Bible and hoped this would also help me to see His will for my life.

I have to say, I am also a bit impatient, if you have not gathered this by my stories here so far. When I pick up a book to read, I like to skim the ending to see where it is leading. I want to know where I am going before I start the ride.

So, in my grand intelligence (*cough, cough*), I decided to read the book of Revelation first. I must give a disclaimer here. I personally do not recommend reading Revelation if you are a new believer. It is daunting at best, with all the visions and apocalyptic times. However, it did scare me enough to know that I needed to take it back a notch and start over. The one thing that stuck with me over the years of reading Revelation first was the last verses of Chapter 22. We win in the end. Thank You, Jesus, for that.

I discovered through my studies that there were many others in history who had wanted their own way, as I had. Some of the hard-bent people were Jonah and his fish, Jacob and his hip, and Samson and his attitude. Again and again, I stumbled upon people who had tried to wrestle with the Lord. I felt helpless in the battle of change. I felt afraid that I might lose myself in the process, like the snow covering a green landscape.

As I read further and uncovered more in the Bible, I began to see God's potential when man steps aside. It is not that God is powerless to move in our lives. He chooses to wait for us. He does not intrude on our free will, but instead patiently waits for us to call on Him. It is our free will that helps us—as well as gets in the way.

Slowly, I began to rely on God more in my daily life, and the Bible became my link to Him. The same words that I could never grasp, years ago, suddenly became clear to me as I dug deeper into the heart and mind of God.

Changes were occurring within me. Writing became my outlet to discover and share my feelings. I started slowly, writing in a journal. Then I wrote these stories. This has been a project of over twenty-five years in the making. The Lord ministers to me while I write and gives me chapters and verses to connect with my stories. We are doing this together. I could not do it without Him.

I have learned over the years that writing is a powerful tool to reach others in faith as well. I saw this when writing the short stories here and sharing them with others. I also saw the power of God when my husband and I wrote for United Marriage Encounter (UME). UME is a Christian-based organization that teaches couples and gives biblically sound advice on communication tools, as well as a weekend alone and unplugged. I will share more about this later.

My husband and I are a speaking team couple and share our stories to help other couples learn communication tools in their marriage. What we share are Band-Aid-ripping stories; however, the deeper we share, the easier it is for the couples to share with each other openly.

The more I write, the more my faith grows as well. The Lord has shown me over the years that change is okay, and that He will always be there for me. He has also taught me many things about myself through the changes in my life. It is a journey, though. The older I get, the more I share openly about my life through writing to reach others and let them know they are not alone. Share your story today with someone. You never know who might need to hear your testimony.

Jeremiah 29:11

"'For I know the plans I have for you,' declares the Lord, 'plans to prosper you and not to harm you, plans to give you hope and a future.'"

I Want to Hear You, Lord

I know I distinctly heard the Lord calling me to walk our dogs one morning. I thought it was a fleeting idea and would go away. Surely the Lord was not asking me to walk the dogs in the morning. Maybe he meant one of the kids should take the dogs out? After all, the kids loved the dogs, and one of them was an early riser in the house. I was not the likely candidate to do this.

I prayed for a while and heard the same message. "Walk the dogs." I could not believe this. I'd have understood if God had asked me to pray for someone, or reach out and speak to someone, as He had done in the past. But walk the dogs? *Well, Lord, I* thought, *if you really want me to walk the dogs... I will.*

The next morning, I awoke to the alarm and was nudged to get up. "Remember, you were going to walk the dogs." Okay, okay... I would start with the one that needed it the most. Carmella was a hyper Brittany Spaniel and *loved* to run and tackle the outdoors. However, her walking skills needed some work. I brought out the leash and started down the street with a very excited puppy. While walking down the street, I noticed that the neighborhood was strangely quiet. Neighbors were just waking, and the normal hustle and bustle of the area wouldn't be until an hour or so later.

I had a relatively hard time controlling Carmella as she pulled constantly on the leash, and made a mental note to purchase a different collar to assist with her new adventure. My concentration level stayed focused on Carmella more than on being up and out at six in the morning. I felt the cool air on my face and focused on the task at hand.

The next morning, I awoke ready to tackle the world. Well, honestly, a little bit more excited than the first day. I had made it one day. This gave me the confidence to continue. I grabbed a leash and called our second dog, Corky, who had a completely different disposition. Corky was a mellow English Springer who was very happy to plod along with anyone at any given pace.

I turned right at the end of our street and headed down the sidewalk. Suddenly, I was aware of the same feeling of quietness that I had felt the day before. It was a quiet, peaceful feeling that led me to pray. I wanted to use the time productively, so I began praying to the Lord about everything. I asked for His peace on my family. I asked for His touch on my neighborhood as I passed each quiet house. This became my quiet time with the Lord.

He wanted me to walk the dogs for me, not for them. Each day could be a time of closeness to Him... a time of sharing with the Lord. I realized that I needed that time to start listening more than speaking.

From that day, I began my mornings with walking one of the dogs and praying and seeking His thoughts for the day. One day, about a week later, I asked to hear the Lord directly. I wondered why I could not hear Him as some other prophets had. I did hear Him in the quietness of my spirit when He spoke to me, but I wanted more. I wanted to hear God like Moses and Joshua did. I began asking the Lord why I couldn't hear Him like they did. I would search my Bible later, after the walks, and found Samuel and Jeremiah, who heard the voice of God when they were younger.

Finally, one day while I sought the answer once again while walking, I felt the Lord speaking to me in the quiet of the morning. "You want to hear me like Moses? Look what Moses went through to have that communication with me." I stopped in my tracks. I guess I had never thought of it like that. Moses had suffered alone for many years until he heard from God. Then I began the list in my head. Others, like Elijah, had suffered and had spent many years alone, with only God to speak to them. Even those like Jeremiah, who had heard from God at a young age, had dealt with persecution because of the messages the Lord had given them.

I guess I needed to look at both sides of this intimate relationship. I did not understand that until He spoke to me. I still ask the Lord to speak to me daily. But I also ask Him to give me the strength to accept what He says.

After that day, walking the dogs became a time of peace for me. Sometimes I would pray for the neighbors as I walked past their homes. Other times the Lord would have me listen quietly to the singing birds in the trees. You cannot get to know someone unless you spend time through talking and listening to them. Take time and listen to Him today. What is He sharing with you?

Luke 18:2-8

"He said: 'In a certain town there was a judge who neither feared God nor cared what people thought. And there was a widow in that town who kept coming to him with the plea,

"Grant me justice against my adversary."

For some time he refused. But finally he said to himself, "Even though I don't fear God or care what people think, yet because this widow keeps bothering me, I will see that she gets justice, so that she won't eventually come and attack me!"'

And the Lord said, 'Listen to what the unjust judge says. And will not God bring about justice for his chosen ones, who cry out to him day and night? Will he keep putting them off? I tell you, he will see that they get justice, and quickly. However, when the Son of Man comes, will he find faith on the earth?'"

Snowball's Chance in a Move

Has God ever used outside influences to speak to or reach you? I thought I knew all the ways God reaches a person. I know you are probably smiling at that statement. Yes, I was young and extremely naïve at the time. Honestly, I am not that much smarter today. I just have more experiences that remind me of how amazingly God works.

Remember Balaam's donkey? This poor donkey was just trying to save Balaam from God's wrath, and Balaam's stubbornness was stopping him from seeing God's direction. I had a Balaam experience with my young family. I judged that God wanted us to stay in the townhouse we lived in together indefinitely, because I was comfortable there. I had no reason to move. God had other plans that would not be revealed for many years from that moment.

We took the kids to the local animal shelter as a field trip one sunny day. The shelter was close by, and we had some free time, and I thought it was a great way for the kids to see some of the animals without making a commitment. They were able to see the barn animals and feed them fancy treats. Then we could go inside and hang with the soon-to-be-adopted cats and dogs. We had done this before, and that day was like any other time that we had gone. Except God stepped in. When we walked inside the building the kids ran all over, wanting to pet and hang with the dogs and cats.

Next thing I knew, there was a white kitten on my lap, and the kids were falling in love. Before it became too much of a scene, we ushered the kids out and started praying about the prospect of becoming pet parents. I reached out to the townhouse rental office and verified that we could have a "pet lease" before making the decision. It was confirmed that we could, and so we drove back to the shelter and picked up the tiny, quiet kitten. He was so small, and the kids immediately named him Snowball. The tiny furball was very quiet and seemed like the perfect pet at the time. This is where it gets interesting. We took Snowball to the vet for a checkup and discovered he was actually very sick and needed medical attention and medicine. The tiny furball was now going to cost more than anticipated. What could we do? Send it back to the shelter? Everyone knew what that meant. So, we decided to step in financially and help the little kitten gain his health back. However, more news was coming.

I reached out to the rental office the next business day and requested the pet lease that I was told we could obtain. I was told that pet leases were not available. Excuse me? I had called in advance to make sure we were in accord with the office regulations. The person I had spoken with changed their mind and refused the lease.

This was like a bad joke. The kids were now praying for the fugitive kitten in our townhouse. What could we do? What was God doing? Had I not listened to Him? After more prayer, we decided to start looking for another place to live. That led to a home builder in the area. They were building starter homes, and the interest rates were so low that the payment would be smaller than our rental payment. This became a no-brainer decision. God wanted us to move and had opened the door to a new home.

This was all because of a tiny kitten named Snowball. God uses all things to get our attention and to move us—sometimes literally. So, next time you ask God for a sign, remember that He can use anything or anyone to speak to you. For us, at that moment in time, it was a very tiny white kitten. What is God using to reach you today?

Numbers 22:28-31

"Then the Lord opened the donkey's mouth, and it said to Balaam, 'What have I done to you to make you beat me these three times?' Balaam answered the donkey, 'You have made a fool of me! If only I had a sword in my hand, I would kill you right now.' The donkey said to Balaam, 'Am I not your own donkey, which you have always ridden, to this day? Have I been in the habit of doing this to you?'

'No,' he said. Then the Lord opened Balaam's eyes, and he saw the angel of the Lord standing in the road with his sword drawn. So he bowed low and fell facedown."

Happy Camper

Whomever made up the term "a happy camper" must have known it was an oxymoron. I seriously believe this, because I am *not* a camper. My idea of camping is a bad hotel with running water and electricity. When I was approached to go camping with my daughter, I thought they had the wrong person. I asked my friend what they wanted me to do at the camp. The choices I had were dishwasher or assistant cook. Camping in the summer heat was not going to be fun in the kitchen. I hated the heat when cooking outside; however, I hated doing dishes by hand even more. So, I chose to be the assistant cook. My daughter was thrilled that I was going. Me, not so much… Well, I attempted to look at the bright side, which would be seeing my daughter and being supportive on her first camping experience. I was also counting on good food while there, since I would be partially responsible for the meals. What could go wrong?

When we arrived at the campsite, I had fleeting thoughts of escape until my daughter got very excited and shouted, "We are here!" I was in for the week. The last time I had been camping was when we lived in Tennessee, over twenty years earlier. There was a reason for that.

We arrived early, which helped me to set up my things before the rush. My obsessive-compulsive behavior started to take over. God is in control, right? But I always try to "help" Him as I organize everything. When we arrived at the first meeting for counselors and staff, I was asked by the director what my "bird name" was. Bird name? Seriously? Without hesitancy, a close friend piped up and said, "'Hawk,' because she doesn't miss a thing!" "Thanks," I replied. I made a mental note to speak with her later. However, from then on for the week, I was dubbed "Hawk." Awesome.

I was assigned a cabin in the middle of the woods. Going back to our previous conversation, I am not a camper. I also have allergies to everything outdoors. I panicked and then decided that if God wanted me there, he would do something about my allergies, or the cabin. Unbeknownst to me, my friend had spoken to the director about my allergies, and they had arranged a different place for me which was so much better. The groundskeeper's house was for me. I slept on a sofa bed and was surrounded by books. I was ecstatic, and she was forgiven for the "Hawk" remark. I also made a mental note to thank Him daily as I stayed there for the week. He is so faithful, even when I complain. He knows what we need even before we ask. That week outside of my comfort zone helped me to hear His voice later. What can you do today to get out of your comfort zone and hear the voice of God?

Matthew 6:26

"Look at the birds of the air; they do not sow or reap or store away in barns, and yet your heavenly Father feeds them. Are you not much more valuable than they?"

Sore Feet and Humbled

Camping can take a lot out of someone who normally finds walking in a park a challenge. I have never been an outdoorsy girl. Remember the allergies? When I was a baby, my mother would place me on a blanket in the grass and walk away, knowing I would never leave that blanket. What we didn't know at the time was that the grass made me itch, and it kept me from straying off of the safe blanket. I would find out years later that I was allergic to a multitude of outdoor plants and trees. I must have known when I was little to just stay on the warm blanket where I would be safe.

Later, as an adult, I had a craving for high-heeled shoes. All kinds of heels. All kinds of colors. Finding the most unique heels became a side passion of mine. I could find shoes anywhere we went shopping, like a bloodhound finds a lost person. I loved wearing the heels everywhere I could. Being only five feet two inches made wearing high heels a bonus. I always joked that I wasn't short, but vertically-challenged. Back in the 80s, I was very tall. I had high heels and high hair! But I digress. Getting to the point, I needed to find a pair of sneakers for camping. I had a pair, but they were dirty and old. I wanted a stylish pair to take with me. I was very happy with my stylish sneakers I had purchased for the trip and couldn't wait to try them out. I left them in the box, nice and clean, until we left.

One of the first mornings while camping, I awoke with very sore feet. I had worn the brand-new sneakers for the first time. I never gave myself or the sneakers the "break-in" time needed. I had thought they would be comfortable because I would be on my feet all day. That is what sneakers do, right? They looked comfortable enough and were very stylish. I didn't have much experience picking out sneakers and discovered that my lack of knowledge was my downfall. For some reason, the shoes were not cooperating with my fashion or my schedule. My feet were so sore, I had to put on my old, dirty back-up sneakers. The new sneakers were over-insulated, and I think I also needed to buy the next size larger. Again, a little background knowledge of sneakers might have helped me earlier. I didn't want to wear the old ones, but the pain in my toes disagreed, so I begrudgingly put on the old pair.

I complained to myself about how stylish I was not at that moment, and how sore my feet were. I carried on the internal grumbling conversation until I saw sweet Marie, who had terrible bunions on her feet, strolling toward me. She walked all over the camp and did everything she could to make everyone happy. When she sat down and took off her sneakers, I noticed she had wrapped her feet to avoid the pressure and pain. I was complaining about my dirty sneakers and my toes, but she never complained once about her feet. In fact, she praised the Lord that she was able to come to this camp for the week. She said that nowhere else could she get a great vacation in a beautiful mountain campsite for a week, free of charge! I surely felt humbled that night. No matter how much my feet hurt, I made the decision not to complain and to look out for her instead. Sometimes it takes a dose of reality to get right back with God and His way of thinking. What is God sharing with you in your daily activities?

1 Thessalonians 5:18

"Give thanks in all circumstances; for this is God's will for you in Christ Jesus."

Matthew 6:16-18

"When you fast, do not look somber as the hypocrites do, for they disfigure their faces to show others they are fasting. Truly I tell you, they have received their reward in full. But when you fast, put oil on your head and wash your face, so that it will not be obvious to others that you are fasting, but only to your Father, who is unseen; and your Father, who sees what is done in secret, will reward you."

Loaves and Fishes – Turkey Style

Helping in the kitchen at camp was not as hard as I thought it might be. Everything seemed to run smoothly, and I was not responsible for any major decisions. Each day seemed to go by quickly as I split my time between kitchen duty, in my fancy apron and hairnet, and spending fleeting moments with my daughter to encourage her first days at camp. We were able to participate in part of the devotional time, which was a blessing and honestly helped me to refocus on why I was there. This was for Him, not for me. At least, that is what I thought. I did not realize He was teaching me a new lesson every day. God surrounded me with a group of elderly ladies who daily humbled my spirit by their willingness to work. Marie was also a volunteer for a local food cupboard. Harriett was a woman of honor who worked hard every day and seemed to be a bit rough on the outside, but had a heart of pure gold on the inside. Jean was a willing servant who spent hours in the kitchen just helping in any way she could, from cutting up vegetables to doing the dishes. Wanda was our head cook. She also had a daughter at camp.

Each day went about the same. Daily activities, cooking, and devotionals. Then, Thursday afternoon came. The head cook, Wanda, told me that she was going to be gone from Thursday evening to Saturday, when camp would be over, and that I was now in charge. "You are joking, right?" I asked, half laughing. She could not be serious. No one had given me a heads-up on this, but she was serious. We were supposed to have a big turkey dinner Friday night. That would be okay, except that I discovered we only had two fifteen-pound turkeys to feed 110 kids and multiple staff members. The burden of how to do that was left to me. I left the kitchen numbly and walked up the stone path to think. "Lord!" I shouted. "What am I going to do?"

I had prayed many times throughout the week that the meals would be served on time and that there would be enough with the small rations on hand. How was God going to help me here? Was I asking too much? "Well, Lord," I started again, "you remember feeding the 5,000 with the five loaves of bread and two fish? I am going to need that miracle here tomorrow evening."

I cried out to the Lord in frustration, not knowing how we were going to do it. That day I had the turkeys prepped, cooked, and ready to go. As I worked diligently to debone the birds, I watched as two tins filled to the top with turkey meat. "These two trays are not going to fill over 100 people, Lord. My faith is smaller than a mustard seed tonight."

The next night, I began to tackle the dinner with prayer. We made a great turkey dinner and heated the meat up in the trays to be ready when everyone arrived. "Lord, I need your help now—please let there be enough for everyone, in Jesus' name, amen." Betty helped me get the turkey onto the trays for the tables.

And then it happened. As we dished out more turkey for each table, the amount in the tins never diminished. The more we dished out, the more turkey there was. In fact, there was enough turkey for people to have seconds! In fact, a staff member came to me later and asked if possibly there was enough turkey for sandwiches to take on their hike the next day. There was enough. There was enough for those sandwiches *and* the staff meal the next day!

I would have never believed it if I had not seen it with my own eyes! Two fifteen-pound turkeys filled an entire camp, and there was extra. "God, you are so good! I have so little faith, yet you still came to meet our needs." I cried that night in thankfulness for the Lord's help. I will never forget how He helped a willing vessel like me, who had little faith to sustain her. What miracles are around you that you might have missed in the busyness of the day?

Luke 17:6

"He replied, 'If you have faith as small as a mustard seed, you can say to this mulberry tree, "Be uprooted and planted in the sea," and it will obey you.'"

The Sheep and a Thief

When the kids were younger, we regularly took trips around the neighborhood after homeschooling for the day. On one occasion, God used a day trip to teach all of us a valuable lesson that still sticks with me. It was springtime, and we were driving by a farm that had brand-new baby sheep all over. In fact, looking at the field, it was covered in white. Sheep everywhere. I slowed down, and the Lord spoke to me. "I care about each and every one of these sheep." How much less could He love me?

I shared these words with my kids in the backseat. "See how God is taking care of these sheep? They are known to go astray, but He keeps His eye on each one of them. He does that for us as well. His eye is never far from us, like a shepherd is never far from his sheep. How cool is that?"

I thought this lesson was over and continued driving. God had other plans. I decided to take the kids to the mall to get out a bit and let them run around the different stores inside. It was an adventure for them. We didn't go to buy anything, but to see what we could discover. Believe it or not, one of their favorite stores was Rite Aid, where they could find so many little items for a small price. They would save up money and then shop around to see what small trinkets they could bring back home. Candy, a small toy–anything that seemed cool at the time. We went through the store and made an adventure of it, and then proceeded to discover the mall's treasures.

As we were leaving the mall, I noticed a scene playing out before us. The kids were buckled in the back of the car as we were heading out. There in front of us was a young man with shopping bags, running from the mall. Behind him were two security guards, running as fast as they could. The young man was darting between cars in the parking lot and heading away from the mall. The security guards were losing ground, as it was not their normal routine to be chasing someone this far. I felt the Holy Spirit speak to me: "Go slow him down." I put the car in drive and drove alongside of him, slowly, and rolled down my window. "Where are you going?" I asked. The young man slowed down, turned around, and had a stunned look on his face. Then he seemed to realize what he was doing again and picked up speed. "What are you doing?" I asked him, as I drove very slowly next to him. I could see the security guards gaining ground as I slowed down their catch. The young man never said anything but seemed perplexed by my questions. God was trying to reach him and was using my voice. He didn't respond, but he slowed down. The guards finally caught up with him, and I then drove off to our next adventure. I spoke to the quiet kids in the back who had just witnessed the scene in front of them. "As God cares for those sheep and what they do, He cares for that young man and wants him to come back home to Him."

When I got home, I opened the trunk of the car and discovered a picture I had left there for later. The picture in the trunk was of a field full of sheep. How prophetic was that? I couldn't have planned it better if I tried. He was speaking to me as well. Yes, Lord. I hear you. Another Holy Echo....

I didn't say anything profound that day, just, "Where are you going, and what are you doing?" It seemed like a small thing at the time, but how profound is it for us today? Where are we going? What are we doing? Who are we doing it for?

Psalm 100:3

"Know that the Lord is God. It is he who made us, and we are his; we are his people, the sheep of his pasture."

Marriage Ministry - God Calls the Unqualified

A few years after I was married, I was introduced to a United Marriage Encounter Weekend. A couple from our church asked if we would like to attend a weekend locally. Having three young children, the thought was very tempting. The couple shared that UME is an incredible ministry that offers a 48-hour unplugged weekend with your spouse, to learn a new tool of communication and practice using that tool. It is for good marriages that want to go deeper. The registration fee was minimal, and being a pay-it-forward weekend, we wouldn't be held back by the financial costs.

Growing up, I was not shown how a Godly marriage should be. Instead, I was taught more of what not to do in a relationship. My motto up until that point was to do the opposite of what I saw around me. I thought it was better than what I had experienced. After accepting Christ, I knew I needed so much more, because my way of doing things was sadly lacking at best. It was like trying to describe a breathtaking sunset to a blind person. I had no idea how awesome a Godly marriage could be. God spoke of marriage in His Word. It would take many years to scratch the surface of what God was saying about marriage and what His plans were. After hearing more about the weekend, I became intrigued and wanted to see what more we could achieve with our marriage together. The couple from our church also offered to assist in finding childcare, and the next thing I knew, we were on our way to a new adventure.

We were so blessed by our UME Weekend, and God showed us how we could make our marriage better through the skills we were taught. The writing we did on our Weekend was intense. I am not going to say it was easy. I had to open up to my husband in a way I wasn't used to doing. I pushed as hard as I could and saw a few breakthroughs that were needed to heal some of the hurts we had been carrying. I wanted to keep this feeling after our Weekend and hoped we could grow more as a couple through what we were taught.

After our Weekend, a couple from the ministry reached out to us and asked if we would like to be a Team Couple. This entails speaking on Weekends and sharing your personal stories so the other couples could share with each other more openly. I remembered the couples who spoke on our Weekend. It was daunting at best. How did they share so much with people they didn't even know? I don't remember jumping in with both feet, but we were once again intrigued with the prospect of helping other couples.

I have to say, I felt unqualified and wondered if they had made a mistake. Didn't they know who we were? Our backgrounds did not really scream "marriage helpers." Instead, it was more like an "avoid what they did" theme. I felt insecure and judged myself too young to speak about marriage. I remember asking God to show us what to do. After prayer, the verse 1 Timothy 4:12 spoke to my heart. I wasn't supposed to look at what I could or could not do in my own strength. He was going to give me the words and the strength. Knowing that I could do all things through Christ, I made the decision to ignore my youth and step out in faith.

The next few years were a blur of writing talks to prepare

for the Weekends, and presenting our stories in front of other couples so they could relate to each other in a deeper way. It was a glimpse into what God can do with two willing but imperfect people. God gave us new friends through the ministry and a new purpose. I felt blessed each time we spoke for United Marriage Encounter, because He was doing the work and I was just showing up. The second blessing was how it strengthened my marriage when we poured into other couples each Weekend. Our cups were being filled as we filled the people in the room. What I didn't know at the time was that God had future plans for me in United Marriage Encounter. I wouldn't discover them for many years. This is another "God story" that I will reveal later.

This story is to share that God can use anyone. Never think that God can't use you, no matter how young or old you are. The Bible is filled with ordinary people He used for His extraordinary purposes. He is just looking for willing vessels. We don't need to be perfect. Just open to what He puts on our hearts. How much more could the Gospel of Christ be shared if only there were more willing vessels? We can move mountains with His help and only a mustard seed of faith. Do you feel unqualified today? Take time to lean into our Savior to hear how He qualifies us.

1 Timothy 4:12

"Don't let anyone look down on you because you are young, but set an example for the believers in speech, in conduct, in love, in faith and in purity."

Forgiveness and Letting Go - Dad's Story

As I walked quietly around my family room, I noticed how colorful each picture of Psalm 100 was. Each of my children had put a personal touch on their project which hung on the walls. These pictures made me think about how God puts His personal touch on our lives.

The house was finally peaceful, with only the droning sounds of the dishwasher in the background upstairs. The radio was softly playing "More of You," as the dogs settled in for the evening. I felt a warm feeling of peace reach out to me.

I should have been thinking about going to bed, because I knew I would regret it if I did not. I have never been an early riser. Yet as I made my way up the stairs to the kitchen and sank into a chair at the table, the peace that filled our home beckoned me to sit and reflect for a while.

It was January 2, and in two more days it would be my father's birthday. What do you get a person when you really do not know them anymore? I had not seen him in fifteen years. "God, help me," I whispered. "I do not have Your wisdom, and I really need it tonight!"

So much had changed over the last year when he came back into my life. His letters, calls, and packages sent a flood of memories back into my mind. Memories I would have rather kept tucked away in a small corner of my mind.

Let me back up a bit.

I bargained with the Lord when I said I would forgive him conditionally, as long as I did not have to see him again face-to-face. Bargaining with God was not only wrong, but highly foolish, when I think about it now. However, five years previously I had sent him a card in the mail. It was a simple card. I had signed it with one sentence: "I forgive you." This small sentence took years to pen.

When I accepted Christ into my life, He began slowly healing my heart and restoring what the locusts had eaten over the many years. What I did not expect was that He also awoke something very deep within my soul. I was so excited to be a new creation, I wanted to reach out to *everyone* I knew! The drive to share the gospel became absorbed into my being. I couldn't wait to share what God had done in my newly-saved life. The thought of holding back my excitement was akin to holding the reins of a team of unbroken horses. I had never had this feeling before and almost didn't know what to do with it.

I started with my family. I reached out to my mother. The thought of her not knowing the Almighty God of love, peace, and forgiveness was too much to bear. I shared my story and felt the Holy Spirit driving my words. After a year of sharing, she accepted the Lord. I was so excited! I also shared with my children whenever I could, until the day they accepted Him as their Lord and Savior as well. I reached out to everyone around me.

When I felt led to reach out to my father, I would stop in my tracks. Him too, Lord? He worked gently on my spirit to forgive my childhood of pain. It took years, but He is a loving God who knew I needed time. "You were forgiven; you need to forgive." I struggled with that concept. I felt immobilized at times. I believed I understood how Jonah felt—the calling, but afraid of the outcome. Over and over, He came to me through Holy Echoes. He came to me in word and song. I would hear it everywhere I went. He was again gentle, but unrelenting. He knew I had to heal here too.

The catalyst was when I came across a book by Corrie Ten Boom titled *The Hiding Place*. For those who haven't read this book—one, you should, just to see inside of a Godly woman in an ungodly world and how she responded. Two, it helps us to understand our history from a personal experience. I felt so much shame reading how she could forgive her captors after all they had done to her. If she could reach out her hand to forgive, then I could as well, with His help. A quick side note here: no one can forgive without His help. It is not in our nature, and especially when it is as egregious as what Corrie Ten Boom went through.

It was time, He told me. So, I went to the store, bought the card, and penned the sentence: "I forgive you." That was the first step. God wanted to take this further. As the letters began to come from my father over the years, I hesitantly responded, with my guard up. Forgiveness does not always mean reconciliation. Only God can do this.

After five years of stepping out in faith, I was told right before his birthday that it was time. I am not going to say I was excited. I was, in fact, petrified. How do I visit someone after so many years have passed? God said He would show me the way.

I am not going to say that this was an easy accomplishment. I am going to say that He called me to do the impossible. However, He met me along the road to healing, and gave me the courage and strength to do what I thought could never happen. Those steps of faith—first, the letter, and second, the visit—were Jonah steps of faith. Remember though: nothing, I repeat, nothing, is impossible with God.

This was not the end of the story. It has continued over the years. I wouldn't find out till years later that my first card gave my father the courage to reach out to God as well. He said that if it wasn't for my card and my reaching out, he might not have forgiven himself and accepted Christ. Stop for a moment and think about that. God not only wanted to heal me, but He wanted my father's heart as well. He stormed the gates to reach him, leaving the ninety-nine to bring my father home. Again, nothing is impossible with God. Cling to that Holy Echo today.

Jonah 2:9

"But I, with shouts of grateful praise, will sacrifice to you. What I have vowed I will make good. I will say, 'Salvation comes from the Lord.'"

Matthew 6:14

"For if you forgive other people when they sin against you, your heavenly Father will also forgive you."

Luke 18:27

"Jesus replied, 'What is impossible with man is possible with God.'"

Prayers for Tires and a Peanut Butter Sandwich or Two

When I finally gave my heart to Jesus, I felt called to tell everyone so they could have the amazing gift I was given. My mother was on the top of my list of people to reach. I judged that she needed Jesus for salvation, and for her personal peace. Growing up an only child in the 40s, with little direction from her unsaved mom, was challenging. Her mother spent many years trying to find her own happiness in the world and through relationships. Mom did not have a solid role model and did the best she could with what she knew. Because she struggled in relationships also, Mom was searching but did not know what she was reaching for.

I spent many of my younger years taking care of Mom and my brother when she divorced. I felt it was my job and took the role to heart. When I accepted Christ, I realized there was someone else that could do much better than my feeble attempts. When Mom finally accepted Jesus, she was so excited and wanted to go where I went again. This was a great story for a bit. We attended church together with the family, and she pressed in to learn all she could while we were together. What I didn't realize is that I had helped Mom to understand the Jesus I knew but had not let her discover her path with Him. She needed to learn who He was to her personally. I was once again trying to take care of her, and now her walk with the Lord. That is when God stepped in.

He has a way of shaking things up when we are stuck in a spot, like going outside and shaking out a rug to get the dirt out. We don't always see the dirt because it is hiding in the crevices, but it is there. When we shake the rug, we are surprised by all the dirt that comes loose. I needed to let God spend time with Mom and not be her crutch in this relationship.

Side note: have you ever tried to get your own way with God? I struggle with this on a regular basis. I want His will in my life, but on my terms. This is like driving down a dark road without headlights. I have a chance of getting there, but it is not going to be pretty.

Mom and I got into an argument one day. Actually, it was more like my expectations of what Mom should have done were crushed, and instead of letting God handle the situation, I harbored resentment in my heart. This resentment lasted an exceptionally long season. We didn't speak during that time, and I struggled with wanting to "fix" it once again. I was told, "No, He needs to work in her life." He also needed to work in mine.

After many months of tears and prayers, He brought her back to me. I felt led to call her, and the woman who answered the phone was a completely different person. She was so excited to share with me what God had been doing. In the most joyful voice, she told me she had lost her job and was going to lose the trailer, but God was in control. Wow... I didn't know what to say at that moment. Speechless, if you can believe it. She began to share the full story. As everything came down around her, God met her in the midst. She used that time to dig deeper into her relationship with Him. She found a church near her and was going to Bible studies and filling all her spare time with the Word.

I cannot even express how overjoyed I was at that moment.

God had not only brought my mother back to me—He had changed her completely and brought me the mother I'd never had. We talked for the longest time. I felt renewed in my spirit as God healed both of us at that time. What transpired next was another plot twist that I could not have made up if I'd tried. Mom began to share with me how God was calling her to move to Florida for a season to help my grandparents. My grandfather's health was failing.

You could have heard a pin drop. I wanted to cry out, "*No!* You can't do this! God, you just brought her back to me. You can't take her away again." He knew what was better. He had plans for her and my grandparents that I didn't know, which were in the making.

What transpired over the next few weeks were "God moments." Mom's faith was so big at that time in her life that she let everything go and just prayed. She had no money to get to Florida from New York. I could not have helped her if I'd tried. I felt so helpless. She prayed for the funds to take the train south. He provided. Someone wanted her old tires in the shed, and she sold them for the exact amount she needed for the train ticket.

I drove her to the train station one incredibly early morning. She had two peanut butter sandwiches in her pockets because she had no money for food on the way. She took her Bible, a suitcase, and those peanut butter sandwiches. She also had God, and a newly acquired faith that moved mountains. I had never been so conflicted. I was so proud of her journey, but so sad to see her go.

Mom's journey would be a long season. God used her mightily to help my grandparents. She would pray over the years there and faithfully listen to His voice. Mom shared Jesus with my grandparents and showed Jesus as she helped them in their struggles. She was the one to pray with them to accept the Lord before they passed. What God did in those moments was nothing short of a miracle. Over the years, I have read many scriptures about training up your children and teaching them about the Lord. God had a different plan for our little family. I would come first, and then He would use me to bring my family to Him. He is so faithful. My prayers today are that I can have the mountaintop faith that my mother had at those moments in her life. Take time today to see what God has planned for you. You won't regret the moment.

Hebrews 12:11

"No discipline seems pleasant at the time, but painful. Later on, however, it produces a harvest of righteousness and peace for those who have been trained by it."

Jeremiah 29:11-13

"'For I know the plans I have for you,' declares the Lord, 'plans to prosper you and not to harm you, plans to give you hope and a future. Then you will call on me and come and pray to me, and I will listen to you. You will seek me and find me when you seek me with all your heart.'"

Luke 17:6

"He replied, 'If you have faith as small as a mustard seed, you can say to this mulberry tree, "Be uprooted and planted in the sea," and it will obey you.'"

School of Hard Knocks

When you are a new Christian, sometimes you feel invincible. Or was that just me? Either way, I was so on fire for the Lord that I couldn't imagine walking away or doing anything that would tarnish my testimony. I felt bold and indestructible, like a skyscraper set in cement. I judged that there was no way I could fail or fall. I was so naïve. I thought I had reached the peak of what a Christian was supposed to be. I judged that I had a solid foundation of God and His Word. I was attending church with the family and hearing from God on a regular basis. My husband and I were in a marriage ministry together. What could possibly make me fall away? There is a scripture verse that comes to mind in this season: "Pride goes before... a fall" (Proverbs 16:18 NIV). Proverbs is a great place to obtain wisdom and to dig deeper with Him. I had never said it aloud, but I judged others in my heart because they had failed while I had not. God knew my heart and needed to help me come to this realization so I could be stronger when I came back.

My first marriage began to crumble in front of me. As I said earlier, I had thought we had it all together. I had found the Lord. We were going to church as a family. We were in ministry together. My life was full, and I believed that my husband's life was full as well, because he had stepped into the arena of fatherhood, which he had been previously robbed of due to infertility. He had chosen to also adopt my children. He wanted this to succeed as much as I did—I thought. I learned over the years that he struggled with many demons I didn't know about at first. The bulimia was first. Next, he was diagnosed with bi-polar disorder.

I felt the heavy blows to my spirit, but being as stubborn as I was, I refused to go down. I was invincible, remember? I fought the battle in my own strength at that time. I believed I could "fix" it again. However, the more I tried to "fix" the marriage, or my husband, the worse things got. What I couldn't wrap my head around was that my husband had to *want* to get better. It wasn't enough that *I* wanted him to heal, physically and spiritually.

When I finally cried uncle, I was down to ninety-five pounds and so far from where I had begun spiritually. My kids came to me one day and said, "We know you don't believe in divorce, but we need to talk." What a sad day that was in my head. I had become my mother. My own children were trying to take care of me. What had happened to me? The mental abuse I had been receiving over the years had hit a button inside of me, and I had returned to the old habits I knew. In my own strength, I chose to step up and move on and help myself. This began a slow journey of walking away from my life and my Lord. I walked away from my marriage, all my Christian friends, the marriage ministry, and my life as I knew it. I was angry, and I didn't feel the love of anything anymore. The more I walked away, the harder my heart became.

I would like to stop here and say that this season was very short. However, it was not. In fact, I became very angry with God about my failed marriage. I walked away from all that I knew and started down another road that God didn't call me to take. I said to myself that I didn't care. But in reality, I yearned for the close relationship I'd had when I first accepted Christ. I judged that the walk back was too far. That was the enemy in my head once again. Without godly advice and being in the Word, I listened to the enemy as he pounded me down, telling me that I was never going to come back.

You might ask why this story is here. I wanted to share it for a couple of reasons. First, I can't do anything without Him. Even when I think I am strong. I am only strong because of Him. This was a lesson I had to learn. Like Peter, who said he would never deny the Lord. The sudden realization when he did was the wakeup call he needed to know that God was his strength. He was not strong without Christ. We are not strong without Christ guiding us.

Second, as far as I ran away, God never left me and tried speaking to me softly to come home. He left the ninety-nine to bring me back. It was an awfully slow process, because I needed to be in the desert for a while to realize what I was missing. That story is coming. If you are in a season like I was, please remember that He loves you and is calling you back to Him. Never think that you are so far away from God that you can't come back home. It only takes one step in His direction, and He is running toward you like the father of the prodigal. Praise God for His mercy and grace. If you are sitting where I was so many years ago, remember that He never gives up on you. Take that one step toward Him. He is waiting.

Luke 22:60-62

"Peter replied, 'Man, I don't know what you're talking about!' Just as he was speaking, the rooster crowed. The Lord turned and looked straight at Peter. Then Peter remembered the word the Lord had spoken to him: 'Before the rooster crows today, you will disown me

three times.' And he went outside and wept bitterly."

Luke 15:4

"Suppose one of you has a hundred sheep and loses one of them. Doesn't he leave the ninety-nine in the open country and go after the lost sheep until he finds it?"

Restoration

Rainbow Reminders & Restoration

What is so amazing about our Father in heaven is that He never gives up on us, even when we give up on ourselves. I put my faith and my walk on hold for a long time. Being a loving Father, He slowly revealed Himself to me over and over during this time.

Even though I walked away, God kept His promise to me and hunted me down. I was very frustrated with myself and everything around me. I started doing everything in my own strength. Work, home, and family were all plugging along, because they don't stop despite my feelings. I felt empty and sluggish as I moved forward, doing the day-to-day activities, looking for peace in my old ways. It was like walking against a massive sandstorm. No matter how hard I fought it, I felt tired inside.

During these times, God would bring rainbows around me to show how He was still working, even though I was astray. These rainbows would be literal as well as figurative. We would have a major storm, and I would walk outside afterward to see a magnificent rainbow painted across the sky. He was quietly telling me He was still here. I would turn the radio on and hear a Christian song. It would bother my spirit, and I would change the channel in frustration. I would still hear the words before I changed the channel, though. Small reminders that He wasn't giving up on me. This went on for a long season. I would see my Bible sitting aside, collecting dust, quietly calling me. Occasionally, I would pick it up and flip through, hoping to obtain a revelation about my situation. I felt cold each time, like stepping outside in winter with the chilling breeze on my face. I thought it was a sign that He didn't want to speak to me. I was playing old tapes in my head of my childhood. What I didn't understand is that He was reaching out to me. I was pushing him away emotionally.

After stumbling along, just getting by, I decided to take a time out and start taking care of me. I had attended college when the kids were younger. I had made it through my first degree and halfway through the second before the world's activities took over, and I had put it aside. I regretted doing that and had always wanted to pick it back up again. It was time to begin again.

I became determined to complete my degree and fix my financial situation. Slowly, I picked myself up and meticulously started down the path of recovery. I pushed hard to clean up my credit and investigated going back to school. Fixing my credit took time. But it was the first step of becoming completely self-supporting. I had plans, but I didn't realize He had plans too, and I was following the path He wanted me on. Once my credit was back in order, I started taking classes. I reached out to my boss at the time and let him know that I was going back to school and wanted to move forward in my career with the company. I pushed myself to work and travel for the company and then do online classes every night and weekend. It was consuming, but I had a goal. I believed that reaching this financial goal would bring me freedom and peace. Again, He had other plans, and I was just on the path He had guided me toward.

Mom was still living in Florida while I was working toward my goals. She wanted to attend church, but could not due to her failing health. I am not sure if it was her idea or mine, but one of us suggested we attend online together. This was the first baby step of faith. We would set up our computers simultaneously to an online service in California, and then I would call her, and we would "attend" together. There were hiccups, but for the most part it went smoothly. We were being fed spiritually together again. He was working in me slowly, using my mother as my guide. How awesome is God to do that?

One day, after one of our online services, I felt the tug to bring her back to New York. Her health was declining, and I knew the writing was on the wall. She didn't have anyone there to help her. She needed me to step in. I mentioned it to her, and instead of saying it wasn't time, she agreed. This was a first, because she had not felt led to leave Florida until that moment. It was time. If I had not been working on my credit, we would not have been able to do the next steps that were needed in our journey.

I hired a mover and flew down to help Mom pack and get ready for her new adventure. We drove all the way back to New York in her little car and had one of our final adventures together. It was crazy, but fun. She had a ball, and I saw the free spirit in her I hadn't seen in years. God used that time to bring us back together and prepare me for the next journey. She settled into our little townhouse and had many plans to move out soon after and work again. I knew God had other plans, so I quietly said, "Okay, Mom." I started seeing why I had been pushed into fixing my financial situation. She was going to need me. He had plans to move me from the townhouse which I had thought I would never leave.

This was the first of the many steps back to Him. Without even realizing it, I was moving back to Him, because I did not feel comfortable on my own. I had been trying to "fit" into a life that I no longer wanted. He was calling me through rainbow reminders and restoration. Go out today and find your rainbows. Dig deeper, and God will reveal Himself to you.

Genesis 9:12-15

"And God said, 'This is the sign of the covenant I am making between me and you and every living creature with you, a covenant for all generations to come: I have set my rainbow in the clouds, and it will be the sign of the covenant between me and the earth. Whenever I bring clouds over the earth and the rainbow appears in the clouds, I will remember my covenant between me and you and all living creatures of every kind. Never again will the waters become a flood to destroy all life.'"

Joel 2:25-27

"I will repay you for the years the locusts have eaten—the great locust and the young locust, the other locusts and the locust swarm... You will have plenty to eat, until you are full, and you will praise the name of the Lord your God, who has worked wonders for you; never again will my people be shamed. Then you will know that I am in Israel, that I am the Lord your God, and that there is no other; never again will my people be shamed."

First House and Mom's Story

As my night school classes progressed and my finances were in order, I wanted to find a permanent home for Mom. After seventy-plus years, she needed a space of her own with us. The townhouse we lived in was perfect for my college daughter and myself. It was no longer perfect with an additional person. Mom needed her space, and I saw the writing on the wall. It was another "Snowball incident." If you don't know what that means, go back a few stories for context. Mom laughed and called herself the kitten that moved us again. She had no idea that God was using her to move the stubbornness inside of me.

I prayed about it and started the process of qualifying for a home. I had never purchased a home alone and honestly didn't know if I would qualify. Sitting on my bed late one night with my laptop, I found a site that prequalifies you according to your credit and income. The next thing I knew, I was staring at a screen that said I could do this. "Really, God? I know you are in control, but can I do this?" Mom was excited when I told her the next morning, and we began the hunt for the perfect home for us.

Backstory here: there was a government subsidy available for first-time homeowners, and I could qualify for that funding. This also made the home market very scarce. We would find a house we liked, and before we were able to even make a bid, it was sold within hours. This went on for weeks. "Well, God, I qualified for a house, but there wasn't one on the map for us." I decided to take a break from the search and told Mom that we needed to get away. Maybe it wasn't our time right now. We needed to wait until the right one was ready.

I decided that we needed to get away. Often, Mom and I would take small, local trips after I brought her to New York. We had not taken a major trip since moving her from Florida. So, one day I asked her, "Where do you want to go? I will book the trip." I left the options open and endless. I had the funds set aside for the house and thought it was time to loosen them and get away instead. I judged that she would pick some exotic place, and I was ready for whatever answer she gave me. "Los Angeles," she said. Seriously? LA? Yes, she wanted to see the stars in the street and do the tourist thing in LA. Well, I have to say that wasn't my first choice, but if Mom wanted to go to LA, then we were going to LA. I packed my schoolwork to do on the road and she got ready with her meds to help her travel.

What I didn't realize was that LA would be our last trip together. I am so glad I gave in to her request without trying to talk her out of it. We had such a good time in a tiny, dingy hotel and doing all the touristy things around town. She loved seeing Jay Leno in person, and we even ate sushi in a beautiful restaurant overlooking the city. It was amazing and so much fun. We rented a car, and her free spirit came out again as I drove the massive highways of LA. She would yell to go faster to get on the onramp and asked to go explore everywhere. It was a moment in time I won't forget.

When we got home, the house for us appeared. The funny story is that it was in the same neighborhood where I had raised the kids and had personally tried to avoid. God, again, had other plans. It was perfect for us and my daughter who was in college.

It was a split-level home on a street called Bluestem Court. My grandmother's favorite color. It was blue with white shutters. The yard was small, but perfect for us. There was a sunroom that Mom fell in love with. She would end up spending many days there, knitting and watching her favorite shows.

I thought we had missed our moment before we left on our trip. I had given up on the idea of owning my own home. However, God was still working on the right house for us. The owner put it up for sale just as we returned from California. I found it by chance, and everything fell into place. If I hadn't listened to His quiet suggestions about my finances, we wouldn't have been able to qualify for our new home. Within months from sitting on my bed stepping out in faith, we were situated in our new home. I saw God work miracles, restoring what the locusts had eaten, as I walked around our new home. I believed this was going to be our new home forever. I had no plans on ever moving again. Everything is for a season. What season has God brought you to today?

Ecclesiastes 3:6, 11

"A time to search and a time to give up...

He has made everything beautiful in its time. He has also set eternity in the human heart; yet no one can fathom what God has done from beginning to end."

Divine Intervention

My husband likes to say that we met in the shower, or online. He enjoys those occasions, sharing how we met. I digress... Let's back up a few years. After going through a couple of bad marriages, doing things in my own strength, I decided I wasn't going to get married ever again. I judged that I had made bad decisions in the past and wasn't about to continue doing the same thing, expecting different results. As I mentioned earlier, I had started back on the track, taking care of myself, the kids, and then my mother by moving her up from Florida. She loved our little house we had moved into, and we had made a great home for everyone in our small family. I felt comfortable that we had what we needed, and I was content being alone.

About four months after we settled into our home, I spoke to a friend and casually mentioned that I might be open to dating again. We laughed at the thought at the time. God took the words to heart. Then the faucet in the bathroom shower stopped working. I couldn't budge the thing, and it was leaking besides. I know software, finance, and project management, not plumbing. God knew that and started the plan in action.

I went online, looking for a plumber to fix the annoying faucet that had taunted me for days. I found a couple of names, and the second one I called answered right away. The man on the other end of the phone was glad to help and said he would come right over. I felt grateful, because I didn't have a lot of time to search for the right one. Work was a bit crazy with traveling, and night school was keeping me occupied with any extra hours I had.

Within a few hours I had a brand-new faucet installed, and I was so excited to find someone who might be able to help with other odd mechanical tasks I might need. I paid the bill and went on my way. The next day I received a call from the same person, and I let it go to voicemail. He was doing a follow-up on his call and wanted to know how the faucet was working. I thought it was a bit odd, but appreciated the full service. He tells people today that he called back to check how my plumbing was doing.

I called back and said it was working fine, and thank you again. He then proceeded to say he hasn't done this before but felt strongly that he should call and ask me out on a date. A date? Seriously? I laughed and said sorry, I didn't date. Remember what I said earlier? I had just said out loud less than a week before that I might be ready. He remained persistent and kept talking for a while and wore me down a bit. He said, "How about we just meet for a drink?" That is harmless, right? Okay, I gave in a bit and said, "Sure, I can do that." He offered to pick me up, but I said no thank you and that I could meet him at the designated spot at the time we chose. He agreed, and the conversation was over.

The backstory, I would find out later, is that after he had left my home the day before, the words "Call her" were in his head for a day, until he could no longer ignore it and said, "*Okay*, I will call her." He thought his guardian angel was speaking to him. Little did he know that the One speaking words to him was much higher in rank.

Well, he was forty-five minutes late for our drink. He called apologetically and mentioned that he had been on a sales call that went over. I was about to cancel the entire evening. But I had decided I was ready to go out, so I opted to bite the bullet and get it over with.

When we finally sat down to talk that night, he spent most of the time talking, as I remained guarded. I found him amusing, though, and I wasn't going to give away that I thought he was cute. We talked for hours. That one night began the start of many dates. Carl had also been through a bit in his life as well. Both of us were basically waiting for the other shoe to drop, and we would then walk away going, yup, not surprised. But it didn't work out that way.

What made me also step back was how our lives were more entwined than I had realized. The more we discovered things about each other, the more we realized that it was not by chance that we had finally met. Carl's birthday was the same day as my grandmother's. The Fourth of July. His kids grew up in the same neighborhood as mine. The ages of our kids were different, but they had gone to the same schools and had the same friends. Our paths had never crossed, all those years, until that one time I called his company. It was time.

My daughter who lived with us at the time was a bit skeptical at best. She was worried about me getting hurt and gave Carl a run for his money. Slowly, methodically, Carl won her over. He doted on her and my mom. I believe Mom liked him more than me after a while. He did everything with them and for them. He was slowly working his way into not only my heart but my family as well. I eventually met his youngest twins and his parents, and we took it day by day. Everyone seemed to accept the two of us as a couple. It happened so slowly, but naturally, that I almost didn't realize how far we had come from that first date.

We continued to take the relationship slowly, and honestly,

it would have been slower if events had not turned the way they did. Again, His hand was in everything. I keep saying this, because what happened next wasn't the way I would have planned. What new gifts has God brought you today? Pray for His revelations.

Proverbs 16:9

"In their hearts humans plan their course, but the Lord establishes their steps."

Mom's Story

When we moved Mom up from Florida to stay with us, I had extravagant goals and plans for our little family. Mom had had a rough life for many years as she dealt with divorce, financial, and personal health issues. The latest blow was side effects due to cancer many years ago. Because her health was deteriorating, I felt called to bring her home so we could help. This would take the financial burden off and help her as her physical health was struggling. As she settled in with us in our new home I had just purchased, I believed we would be there for many years to come. God had other plans.

I met Carl, as mentioned earlier, and we began the very slow process of getting to know each other. I didn't have any future plans at the moment with him—only to get out occasionally for company outside of the daily routines. He was a welcome distraction.

Mom and I had attended church online because of her health before she moved up. We continued that process when she moved in. I did this for her. My walk was shaky at best, due to everything I had been through since my first divorce. I believed that God was real. I had seen miracles. I had heard from Him many times when I first believed. I've shared them with you in my earlier stories. However, after my first divorce, I had stepped away because I had felt so hurt over everything. I basically took a time out from Him. I didn't feel His presence during those years. I felt alone and forced things to work in my own strength. It was a desert experience for me. The problem was that I had created that desert, not God. He was there all along. Going to church online was for Mom. It was a chore to go see Him, because I didn't think He could ever forgive me for all that had happened during those years. How could I come back from where I had started? I kept my distance.

Mom went in for surgery just under a year after I met Carl. It was supposed to help with all the complications the cancer had caused. It was the beginning of a very long season in our lives that lasted eight months. After the first surgery she recovered slowly, and her personality began to change. She started forgetting simple things. It was slow at first, and it then increased—along with her impatience with me. She loved when Carl or my daughter came to visit. They could do no wrong. I was so frustrated and wanted to fix her. I tried everything in my own strength.

Mom went into the hospital for the second surgery after five months. This one was harder on her body than the first. The complications began increasing. So did the miracles. God used that moment in time to bring back one of my sons, who had been a prodigal for over six years. He was able to see Mom and spend time with her before she got worse, physically and mentally. I saw a small glimpse of His mercy as He gave my mom comfort in seeing her grandson at Easter.

Things took a turn a few short months later. I spent many hours taking her back and forth to the emergency department and fighting with nurses and staff to get her the care she needed. I would sit in her room for days with my laptop, doing work as we waited for better results. They never came.

I got the call in the wee hours of the morning. They told me to hurry, and that it wasn't good news. Carl came with me.

I felt so helpless and could only cry. I asked Mom in the ICU if I could pray for her. She could only nod because she had been intubated. I prayed such a feeble prayer and never felt so helpless, just watching her. I wanted to be so strong for her and just kept telling her it was going to be okay, and she would be fine. The doctors gave her meds for the pain. My daughter drove five hours from college, and Mom hung on until she arrived. Time stood still at that moment. We all stood around her and just cried for hours.

As I write this, my heart breaks all over again. My biggest regret is that I waited to come back to Him until after she passed. My thoughts haunted me. I could have given her more peace and prayer than I did in the end. What kind of daughter was I? I ran over and over in my head what I could or should have done to make it better. The enemy was taking that moment to try and completely crush me. The Lord used it to reach out and tell me to come back home. Don't wait to come back if you are holding back. He is calling you too. Step into His presence and dig deeper. He will meet you where you are.

I also had to wrap my head around the fact that God was calling Mom home. It was her time. I struggled with that fact for a long time. No matter what I did or could have done, it wasn't going to stop her season from ending. Nothing was going to stop His timing. He had a plan for her to be with Him where there was no more pain or disappointments. He also wanted to push forward a plan that He had for me.

Carl stood by me through it all. He never said anything. He didn't have to. He was just there, like the rock I needed at the time. He wept with me and never left my side. Afterward, he helped me plant a tree in her name in front of our little home. I could only sit and watch as he dug the hole and planted the tree. God used Carl to help my healing.

He stayed with me from that moment forward. Four months later, he asked me to marry him on my birthday. I was ready. I would not have been ready earlier. It was time to move on and come home. God was quietly whispering to me. Is this a season of change for you? Never give up—and cling to our heavenly Father, who will never let you go.

Ecclesiastes 3:1

"There is a time for everything, as a season for every activity under the heavens."

Luke 15:17-18

"When he came to his senses, he said, 'How many of my father's hired servants have food to spare, and here I am starving to death! I will set out and go back to my father and say to him: Father, I have sinned against heaven and against you.'"

Coming Back Home...

I spent quite a few years conquering school and finding the right job in my own strength. The accomplishments were made, but they were a bit hollow. I had judged that the little I did to come back to my faith was not enough to gain His favor. What is sad, like Peter discovered in the Bible, is that Jesus is always waiting for us to come back. It only takes one step. There is no magical formula of what we need to do. We just need to turn and look up. He helps us do the rest.

God delivering Carl to me was a turning point of looking up once again. God was nudging me to turn everything over to Him. I heard the Holy Echoes in my heart over and over, calling me to Him. I knew Carl was part of this plan but was not sure where. My husband was like no other man I knew. His dedication to everything he did was refreshing, and his drive in his business paralleled my drive at work. I judged that we were in unison with our work ethics. However, I knew we were not equally yoked together with God. Carl believed in God but had not accepted Him into his heart. We were compatible, which helped get everything done, but again we were two different people. The problem with marriage is that it consists of two very broken people who carry their own baggage to the table. Both my husband and I had baggage from previous relationships, and that caused disagreements over how we dealt with different issues. These disagreements became more regular than I wanted, and the disillusionment grew stronger.

There were a few loud discussions in our home, and I felt disillusioned, like I had invested everything I had into a "can't lose deal" and had suddenly found the small print of exceptions. That was the moment God stepped in and said, "Hold on to Me." I needed to refocus my eyes on Him and release my husband into His arms. I could not have a meaningful, open relationship with my husband unless I opened and renewed my relationship with my heavenly Father. The more I heard the call to come sit at His feet, the deeper the need became to let go of myself.

In frustration, I would cry out to Him over the arguments. The song "Need You Now" by Plumb captured my frustration and turned me toward Him. The realization that I needed to make God first, no matter what, grew clearer in my mind daily. I would not have complete peace without making Christ number one in my heart over everything else, including my husband.

The final moment was when I heard a song by the artist Crowder playing one day. "Lift Your Head, Weary Sinner" kept catching my attention. As I listened to the lyrics,

"If you're lost and wandering
Come stumbling in like a prodigal child
See the walls start crumbling
Let the gates of glory open wide,"

I could hear Him calling me back into His will. I visually saw a beaten-down individual, barely standing, pushing open massive oak doors with all his might. I was that person. It was time for me to stop fighting and come home to my heavenly Father. I heard the song over and over. I then wrote the words down and reflected on them. That was me. The prodigal daughter, who thought there was no path back to my heavenly Father. The Holy Echoes reached my heart, and I recommitted my life to Him at that moment and made the decision to keep God first in my life over everything else. It was like the heavy chains that were holding me back fell from my body, and I suddenly felt free again.

I am not going to say that the relationship with my husband instantly changed. It is still a work in progress. Things that are broken take time to fix. God continues to work on me and on my husband. I am going to say that I learned that day that He needs to be my priority, no matter what. The more I put God first in my life daily, the more peace I have with anything that comes at me physically or spiritually. He reminded me that He had never left my side, and that I am a daughter of the King of all kings. Because I am set apart by His grace and holiness, I can stand in faith, knowing whose child I am. I am also more aware of who I am in my own strength. I am nothing without Him and can fail at any time without His help. I have a new revelation of who I am not. I am imperfect and in need of my heavenly Father's guidance every day. I need to empty myself of my will and ask for His will in my life daily.

This was freeing to me, because I realized that I do not have to be perfect. There is only one perfect One. He is working on me every day to become more like Him. I will not be completed until I am with Him face-to-face. So today, I am basically one beggar telling another where to find food. The food is the Bread of Life.

Always remember: You are never so far from God that you can't come back as well. That one step back can change everything and bring clarity to your soul. You can start over every day with His grace and mercy. Praise God for that!

Luke 15:18-20

"I will set out and go back to my father and

say to him: Father, I have sinned against heaven and against you. I am no longer worthy to be called your son; make me like one of your hired servants.' So he got up and went to his father. But while he was still a long way off, his father saw him and was filled with compassion for him; he ran to his son, threw his arms around him and kissed him."

Romans 8:1-2

"Therefore, there is now no condemnation for those who are in Christ Jesus, because through Christ Jesus the law of the Spirit who gives life has set you free from the law of sin and death."

Carl's Story - Marriage Ministry, Take Two

I distinctly remember the day God told me that we needed to go on a United Marriage Encounter Weekend. I also remember my answer. "*No*, Lord. Remember what happened the last time I went on a UME Weekend? It turned out so well, remember, Lord?" I am sure that God found me slightly amusing as I stood up on the inside again and loudly said, "*No.*" I proceeded to share with Him how my past failure with UME had produced no fruit, and tearing that Band-Aid off was not a plan in my future. I had left that life behind almost twenty years before and had no desire to relive it again. I didn't want to see those people again. I did not want to walk in as the failure I judged that I was. God had other plans. He had plans for my husband, and He also had plans for me.

I was told by the Lord that my husband would be saved on the Weekend. I still said, "*No, Lord.*" I know it sounds selfish and contradicts what I had been praying for over the years. He was quietly working in me at that moment. Since the day I had recommitted my life to Christ, I had yearned for Carl to know Jesus personally, like I did. Coming back to the Lord woke something up within me that had been asleep for so many years. It was like waking a sleeping giant. God knew more about me than I did about myself at that time. Doesn't He always? I wanted others to have the joy that I had, once again. I was reaching out to everyone again and sharing more and more each day. God knew I was ready, even though I didn't see it.

What I also didn't realize was that God had been preparing Carl's heart. Carl had been searching for God over the years and had never realized that He was speaking directly to him. Carl would say it was his guardian angel. He would receive direction on how to accomplish a task in the middle of the night. I knew who was speaking to him. He was having a Samuel experience and didn't even realize it. How awesome is God that He reaches down to us when we are lost and picks us up where we are, to place us in the path He has planned for us? He had plans for Carl. I needed to be obedient.

When I gained the courage to ask him if he would like to go on a United Marriage Encounter Weekend, he said, "Sure." I had really expected him to say no. I was stunned. So, what should I do now? I asked him if he knew what it was about, and he said, "Yes." He had been on a different denomination Weekend many years before and vaguely recalled the event. So, again in obedience, I signed us up. I thought maybe he would change his mind or work would get in the way. Remember, we would be "unplugged" for forty-eight hours. Neither one of us had been unplugged from work in many years.

There is another side story here. What you don't realize is that Carl may have attended a Weekend, and he knew at that moment that I had too. However, he didn't know the rest of the story. He didn't realize how involved I was in UME and that I was part of a Team Couple who spoke on Weekends. I had kept that close to my heart, because I felt ashamed to even share that incredible failure in my life. I thought I would just take him on the Weekend, God would do His thing, and we could go on with our lives from there. I know I should have shared this with my husband. I should have trusted him with this information, but I was scared.

On our Weekend we sat in the car before going into the building. I told my husband he could change his mind. He didn't and said it was fine. So, I mustered all I had and walked into the building with my husband. Like a splash of cold water on a hot day, I was met by couples who I knew. Not only did I know them, but they were ones I had presented Weekends to many years ago. These couples from my original Weekends were now Team Couples and sharing their stories with other couples. I was so conflicted and didn't know whether to cry or run away. One of the women came up to me and quietly spoke to me. "Do you remember me?" I said, "Yes." She said, again quietly, "I am so happy to see you." Again, I wanted to break down, but I had the entire Weekend ahead of me. So, I mustered a quiet "Me too" response and sat down. A couple more people came to us and said the same thing. At that point, Carl was looking at me like, "What am I missing here?" I brushed it off for the moment and decided that the cat was out of the bag, so to speak, and I would have to share the rest of the story later.

As we went through our Weekend, my husband and I shared more than we ever have with anyone in our lives. We were both ready for this time. We opened up to each other in a new way through the skills the Team Couples taught us. I recalled how awesome the tools were before in my life and dusted them off to bring new life to our marriage.

I then saw God reach Carl on Sunday morning. Couples were sharing at breakfast about how God had orchestrated how they had met. Carl could not deny it anymore and later, in our quiet room, accepted Christ into his heart. Carl suddenly realized that all those times he had thought it was his guardian angel speaking to him, it was God Himself speaking life into his heart.

What an amazing revelation for my husband. Being a part of that moment was an incredible blessing for me. I have never been more joyful and wanted to shout it out to everyone.

God had brought me Carl after so many years of pain and struggles. He then took Carl where he was and brought him to the cross. Once there, Carl was never the same again. You couldn't hold him back. Wild horses couldn't hold him back. He was on fire for the ministry. He wanted to do it all. Right before we left the Weekend, Carl told me he wanted us to be a Team Couple. *Seriously, Lord? Not amused.* That would be too much for me. I wasn't ready. This would be another story.

God spoke to Carl that Weekend and met him there. God healed old wounds for me that Weekend and met me there as well. He had plans that I never saw. He wanted us on the same page and moving forward with His plans. We walked away from that Weekend equally yoked and began the process of learning what He wanted for us as a couple. Do you have wounds that need healing? Reach out to the greatest Healer today! He will meet you there.

1 Samuel 3:10

"The Lord came and stood there, calling as at the other times, 'Samuel! Samuel!' Then Samuel said, 'Speak, for your servant is listening.'"

New Business Adventures

Who gives up a job for a pay cut and puts all their eggs in one basket? Well, I would question it if someone came to me with that statement. However, I did not plan on doing it personally. I am a logical person who works with facts and numbers daily. I spent many years in school to obtain a good job so I could take care of the family. Some of those school years were when the kids were small, and again after they were out of the house in college. I needed to use our time and finances wisely, and was proud to have graduated with honors, and then to achieve another certification three months later. I knew that every hour I spent studying would come back financially if I achieved the degrees. After many years of school, I moved forward in the corporate world. I loved what I did and pushed hard every day to get ahead in my job. After over ten years in the software industry, I was a bit disillusioned. The paycheck was awesome; however, the personal satisfaction was not there. I was traveling monthly, and it was taking a toll on me. I had convinced myself that every job would have the same stress levels and just kept plugging through.

Then my husband accepted Christ, and our entire lives moved in a different direction. We had jokingly mentioned me working in his business. I say jokingly, because I was not serious about the change; however, he felt differently. My husband knew that with my experience, we could join forces and move the business into the next level. I was very reluctant to make the leap, because the money I was making in the corporate world was my security blanket and I had worked too hard to get where I was. The money I made helped to paid for bills and the extras. I could not imagine making even close to the same amount in the business. It could not sustain my additional payroll and honestly, I did not want to burden the business or my husband with an additional employee. Remember putting all the eggs in one basket? I am not a gambling person.

Well, when God has other plans, and when you do not listen to your spouse speaking through Him, things happen. My job started to become more difficult. There was tension that I could not fix. Things became harder and harder to let go. I heard once that an eagle will get her young to leave the nest by pulling out feathers one at a time until the baby feels the wood and becomes uncomfortable by the poking and finally leaves the nest. I am not sure how true that is. (I did look it up. Do not do that unless you want to go down the Google rabbit hole of birds and their habits.) Either way, that is a good analogy of what God does with us. Little by little, He can make things uncomfortable until we move forward in the direction He is guiding us. Remember Jonah? I do not pretend to be a great prophet like Jonah. However, He got my attention after all the feathers were removed from my proverbial nest.

I became so frustrated in my job that I finally came to my husband and asked that we pray about my job and possibly leaving it to come home and work in the business. I am sure God was amused by me. I am a bit headstrong. After so many prayers and a huge step of faith, I gave my notice. The step was huge to me, but only a curb for my husband. He knew and had faith for both of us at that time. I resolved that if it did not work out, I could move to another job fairly quickly. That gave me the courage to move forward.

When I came home and started the process of changes in

the business, my goals were so much bigger than my paycheck. I started moving our company into the digital world. We went paperless after thirty-plus years. That, in layman's terms, means that we began the process of using software for our scheduling, estimates, and invoices. Change can be painful, and this one was for our team. My husband and I had a few "loud" discussions over the months. However, God is good, and we can say we made it through. The amount of positive feedback we currently receive with all the changes made is amazing.

Fast-forward to today: God has moved mightily in the business. I have not had to find another job. I am not earning what I made when I left the software industry, but I am making a decent income, and the business has increased by over 60 percent. This is after only a few years. I cannot wait to see what God will do in the coming years with our business. We have less stress because I am not traveling all over the US like with my last job. We have been able to participate in United Marriage Encounter because I am working from home. God knew the plans. I just needed to trust. Is there a leap of faith you need to make today? What is God telling you today? Is there a change He is asking of you? Trust me, it is easier to just listen and obey. I know from experience. As I often say, take my advice—I am not using it. I am learning, though. I am a project in process. I have discovered that it is better to listen and trust Him instead of my own thoughts. Are you stepping out in faith with God's direction? You can do it without fear, knowing that He will always be by your side.

Proverbs 1:7

"The fear of the Lord is the beginning of knowledge, but fools despise wisdom and instruction."

Your Body is a Temple

I love food. I love to cook and absolutely enjoy feeding those around me. Often, if you come to my home, you will be fed whether you are hungry or not. My kids knew that and so did their friends. When one came to visit, I would find a way to feed them. Snacks, leftovers, whatever I could find in the fridge. I was the feeder in the neighborhood. Years later I would send our grown kids home with food, just in case they did not have enough food at their home. I did not think it was a bad thing. It was how I showed my love.

Food was a comfort for me growing up. I learned at a young age that dairy was not too fond of me. I loved ice cream, whole milk, and cheesecake. Not at the same time, obviously. However, they were some of my favorites. Each time I consumed any dairy, my stomach chose to voice its opinion, and after a while I decided that it was easier to avoid the milk products than to suffer the repercussions. The aftereffects—well, let's say they were not table talk. So, I stayed away from dairy for the most part. Even though I *loved* cheesecake. I chose to direct my way to the other desserts instead and avoided the creamy delicacy that was calling me. Did I mention that I love cheesecake? Sorry, I digress.

As I got older, I noticed that my body was not happy with other foods I ate. I knew that dairy was a no-no because again, my stomach did not appreciate the ice cream as much as I did. Fast food became a love/hate relationship because of its side effects as well. So, I tried multiple fads to eat healthy and lose some weight. I judged that if I ate healthy, the pain in my stomach would go away. After a while, my stomach was not happy with just about anything I ate. This is frustrating for someone who loves to eat as much as she loves to cook.

I went to a friend who was also a medical professional. After blood work and discussions, she told me that I should give up sugar, gluten, and dairy. She said they were hurting me more than helping me physically. Those foods were causing inflammation in my body, which in turn was causing the pain. I smiled and nodded, and then when I left, I picked up a burger on the way home. Give up pasta and bread? What craziness was that? I knew someone who had attempted to give up bread years before, and I saw her fail miserably because everything we liked was made of wheat. I was not going to be one of those statistics.

After struggling with pain for a few more years, I finally cried uncle. The pain of change was less than the pain of staying the same. I had asked God to take away the pain for years. Sometimes I forget that He uses others to give me the solution, and my friend was the solution. I am a bit stubborn, and it took being in constant pain to finally give in. I decided that the only way I could do this was to go cold turkey.

I would like to say that giving up those foods I loved was easy. I judged that it would be relatively easy because I did not eat much sugar, and I had stayed away from all dairy products. What I had not realized is that wheat and gluten products have sugar in them as well. That is where I was consuming most of my sugar, without realizing it. The first week without any gluten and sugar was a whole new level of "are you kidding me?" My husband attempted to join me in my venture. He lasted about a week. Change is not for the fainthearted. I plugged through and tried not to get too angry when he ate pizza in front of me. This was my battle, not his.

Months passed, and I noticed that not only did my stomach stop hurting, but other things became more noticeable. The weight that I had been struggling with also went away. One day I was driving down the road, and I noticed that the view ahead of me seemed more blurry than normal. I kept squinting and blinking, thinking it was just fatigue. Finally, I took off my glasses and realized that I could see better without them than with them on. What craziness was that? I thought I was losing my mind. I made an appointment to get my eyes checked. My eyesight had reversed. My prescription was one half of what I had needed two years before.

The inflammation in my body was so intense previously that it had affected even my eyesight. I called my friend who was in the medical field and shared the news. She was extremely excited, and I was very apologetic that it took so long to listen to her. My stubbornness to listen to advice slowed my learning process.

I would like to say that I am still on the straight and narrow all the time. But we both know that would be a lie. I am human. I still fall back into old patterns. However, when I do, I see the drastic changes in my body and go back to what is better for me. God wanted to show me that my body was a temple for Him. Not just my mind. I cannot help others if I am not healthy. What can you do today to heal your temple that God created?

1 Corinthians 6:19

"Do you not know that your bodies are temples of the Holy Spirit, who is in you, whom you have received from God? You are not your own."

Philippians 4:13

"I can do all this through him who gives me strength."

Sir Obadiah Rocco & Sir Amariah Benny

When I met my husband, he had two puppies sharing his home. I thought they were cute; however, I had no intention of taking on any more obligations. I had owned dogs growing up, and the two dogs from my first marriage we'd had to adopt out due to financial and living arrangements. It broke my heart, and I never wanted to go through that pain again. God has a sense of humor, because not only did my husband have the two dogs, but he also had four kids. When you added this to my three, we suddenly became the "Brady Bunch." I remember when I was younger saying that I was never going to have kids and live in the city by myself. I am sure that God laughed at my statement. One puppy was not with us long because she wanted to be the only pet in the house, so we adopted her out to a single woman who could give her all the attention. The other dog was officially my husband's pet; however, after I became part of the family, the puppy also adopted me.

Onny was a black Shih Tzu, and a tiny one at that. She was a whole five pounds and had a great personality. She loved to hang out on the back of the couch or on pillows and blankets like a queen. She followed me everywhere and sat in the overstuffed chair next to my desk as I worked daily. She became part of my work routine and never left my side. Then one summer day, not so long ago, Onny got sick. As hard as I tried to help her, she decided it was time. I was crushed. I remember crying out to the Lord, "It wasn't even my dog!" as I wept, sitting on the porch.

We laid her to rest in the front garden where she loved to hang out most. I decided then and there that I was not going to get another animal, period. It was too painful. My husband had other ideas.

Over the next few months after Onny passed, my husband would get creative and take pictures of customers' cute puppies while he was on site and then send them to me. I ignored the pictures, but eventually they got to me like a small stone in my shoe. It created a new desire deep within. I wanted a puppy again. So, we went online and found a Maltese named Rocco that I fell in love with at first sight. He was a pure white fluffball about six months old and six pounds.

(I must back up a bit again here. Normally, I would have looked at the local shelters for a puppy; however, with my numerous allergies, I had to look for a dog that would be basically allergy-free. My selection was slim with my allergies and left only a few choices that were not available locally.)

I met our new puppy at the airport terminal and gently took him out of his crate. He immediately clung to my neck and would not let go. He decided he'd had enough of the crate and the trip. I didn't blame him, so I proceeded to bring him to his new home attached to my shoulder. I was thankful that the ride was short, and the puppy was small. I am sure we were quite the sight to other cars driving next to me.

I named him Sir Obadiah Rocco, because he became God's servant to heal my heart from our little Onny. Rocco followed me everywhere, which was again a blessing. The hard part was that he only bonded with me and did not choose to socialize with anyone else, including my husband. It was a rocky start with poor Rocco, and to be honest, he almost ended up back on the plane. My husband was used to all dogs loving him. He could not imagine a puppy not wanting to spend time with him.

It took a *lot* of patience and work, but the two became friends after a long season of training and treats. God used that moment in time to teach my husband that some things are worth working a bit harder for. He did, and the result was a rocky but steady relationship between the two.

A year or so after we had Sir Obadiah Rocco, I felt strongly that God was speaking to my heart that Carl needed a puppy too. Rocco was my dog, no matter how hard I tried to get him to acclimate with anyone else. I felt inspired by our heavenly Father that my husband needed his own companion, even though we were so busy with our jobs. I laughed at the thought, because that also meant twice the work and messes.

Working from home made it easier to care for Rocco and his clinginess. But another puppy? God had to know that it was going to fall on me to take care of them both, since Carl would be out of the house most of the day. Eventually, my instinct to get a new puppy was stronger than the concern over the mess. So, I went back online and found a Shih Tzu puppy named Benny. I then went to my husband while we were away on a trip and said, "You need a Benny," as I showed him the picture. He laughed at my comment and brushed it off. I was convincing though, and after the weekend we started preparing for Benny to come to our home.

Benny came by bus messenger from out of state. We thought this would be better than the plane ride poor Rocco had experienced. When the messenger showed up one late night, she brought a very tiny multicolored fluffball to my door. I took the tiny puppy and gently handed him to my husband. Benny was about the size of my husband's large, burly hand. The puppy was so excited to see my husband that he immediately began licking his face uncontrollably. The bond was set.

I named him Sir Amariah Benny, because I believed Benny was promised by God to Carl. Benny settled into our routine like a pro and became Carl's best friend. When Benny hears my husband's truck come down the driveway, he jumps up and runs to the door as the truck beeps while backing up. He looks at me quizzically, like, "I don't have opposable thumbs and could use a bit of help here with the door." The minute the truck stops, I open the door, and Benny runs out of the house full speed with Rocco at his side. He knows that his Dad is here, and the routine licking of the face will commence. Carl cannot go far without Benny close behind. Benny has to say good night to Carl before he scoots to my side to sleep. I only think he sleeps on my side because Carl tosses and turns, which can be a bit dangerous for the puppies. The puppies believe in safety first, after kisses.

Rocco has also changed since Benny became part of the family. We tried all sorts of training and acclimation for Rocco. When Benny arrived, Rocco suddenly became part of the daily greeting event. He wants to run to Dad as well, and get picked up to say hello at the end of the day. Rocco needed a Benny too.

God showed me, through these small balls of fur, unconditional love. He reminded me that we are loved unconditionally by Him as well. We are blessed to have a loving Father who can love us so much more than our Rocco and Benny. Each puppy loves us with all his heart; however, our heavenly Father's love is so much more. So much so that He gave His Son to spend eternity with us... How awesome is that thought? We didn't realize we needed a Benny to bring new life into our home. God brings us blessings daily, and sometimes they are shaped like tiny fur balls. What animal or person has given you a God lesson?

John 3:16-17

"For God so loved the world that he gave his one and only Son, that whoever believes in him shall not perish but have eternal life. For God did not send his Son into the world to condemn the world, but to save the world through him."

Get Ready - Jeremiah 29:11

My husband and I took time off from the business to go attend a United Marriage Encounter event for training and fellowship. We love going to these events, because they bring joy to our spirits as we reconnect with other like-minded couples who have a stake in each other's marriages. Another blessing is that often, God meets us there with either a word or a blessing through the fellowship with other couples.

At this particular event, I was given two words: "Get ready." It came quietly when the weekend started and slowly grew louder as the days passed. "Get ready." Like a Holy Echo, no matter what I was reading or sharing, I kept hearing the words "Get ready." When the weekend was just about over, my husband and I went up for prayer. I wanted to know: what are we getting ready for? The pastor who prayed with us shared the scripture from Jeremiah 29:11. He has plans for us. I felt confirmed by the word, but a bit confused as well. Again, what were we getting ready for?

I am a detailed person and I want as much information I can capture when given a task. Can you relate? Often, God will give us a direction to go, but not always the entire map. It is a walk of faith as we trust that He has our best interests in mind and knows that we need to take direction one step at a time. Honestly, if I had known ahead of time what God had planned for me over the past years, I might have run the other direction faster than Jonah could hide in the belly of the ship, away from Nineveh.

He knows me so well. Psalm 139 reminds me of that knowledge. I regularly put it in birthday cards for friends and family to remind them of how much He knows and loves them. Psalm 119:105 was shared with me many years ago. His Word is our daily guidance through life. As a lamp shows only a partial view in the darkness, we are shown each step—where to place our foot as we walk in faith. He gives us exactly what we need to know at the right time. He is a God of "just in time." I often struggle with that thought, because I am a project manager by trade and as mentioned earlier, I crave the entire game plan in order to move forward.

The words "Get ready" were spoken to me that weekend. I had no idea that within months, the entire world would be changed by a small word: COVID. I had no idea that my entire world would be rocked by something we had never seen in our lifetime. I just knew that I needed to get on my knees and pray as I got ready. If I had known that day what was really coming, I might have made different choices. Not necessarily better choices. Decisions would have been made in haste or fear. He wanted me to make His choices, so I patiently waited for the "rest of the story," so to speak, as Paul Harvey used to say. I am grateful for a loving God who not only hems me into Him but prepares me by speaking two small words into my heart. "Get ready." Trust the process, and trust our loving Father, who knows the beginning from the end. He will guide your steps.

Psalm 119:105

"Your word is a lamp for my feet, a light on my path."

Psalm 139:1-6

"You have searched me, Lord, and you know me. You know when I sit and when I rise; you perceive my thoughts from afar. You discern my going out and my lying down; you are familiar with all my ways. Before a word is on my tongue you, Lord, know it completely. You hem me in behind and before, and you lay your hand upon me. Such knowledge is too wonderful for me, too lofty for me to attain."

Elusive Sleep

How many times have you woken up in the middle of the night and were unable to get back to sleep for minutes, or even longer? Some people are blessed with a good night's sleep that carries them to the next morning, refreshed and ready to tackle the world. Sadly, I am not one of them. I do have a system. My nightly ritual includes taking some melatonin to assist in the process and praying before I fall asleep. Normally, it does not take long for me to drift off after praying. However, after a few hours I find myself staring at the ceiling as the puppies and my husband sleep peacefully next to me. At that moment, my mind takes over and starts its own marathon of daily activities.

On the topic of sleep, I purchased a step tracker that also monitors my sleep patterns. I do question my purchase, because I now fixate on how much sleep I did or did not get each night. That obsessive-compulsive nature kicking in again. Here is a quick lesson on sleep trackers. The one I own gives four stages of your sleep during a night. Deep sleep, light, REM, and awake time. I am a bit competitive and try to beat not only my thirty-day averages, but the benchmarks which compare me to women my age. I like to compare days and sleep patterns each morning.

The stages that plague me the most are deep sleep and awake time. I have noticed that if my deep sleep is within a specific zone, I feel better the next day. If I am tired in the morning, I check to see how long I was awake during the night. No comments on being a morning person, please. We both know at this point that I am not!

So, after all this, what I really wanted to share were the moments when I woke in the middle of the night. Again, the OCD in my brain tends to go into overdrive. I begin to relive all that I have said and done during the day. I then start to criticize myself on how I said something, or how I could have said it better. I know—this is not necessarily a productive evening, and the results increase my blood pressure and make sleep harder to grasp.

One night I was in a turmoil state of rehashing the day, and I called out to the Lord. I often recall scriptures to help calm my thoughts. Scripture was not working that night. I asked God to help me sleep and slow down my thoughts. The next thought that came to my mind was: there is no condemnation for those who are in Christ. I knew that one but could not remember where it was. I sat on it for a minute. This is a truth that I can cling to. There is *no* condemnation for those who are in Christ. So, whatever I did or said, it is covered by the blood of Christ. If He could forgive me, then I needed to forgive myself. I am a work in progress. I am nowhere near where I should be; however, I am moving forward in Him. He often speaks to me at night when everything else is quiet. I need those times to hear Him clearly. That scripture gave me peace that night, and on other nights afterward. I'm hoping it will for you as well.

Another thought was given to me by a good friend: "Maybe you are awake because God wants you to pray for someone." Wow—I had not thought of that one before. So, the next time I woke up, instead of getting frustrated, I turned my palms up to Him and asked who I should pray for. The next thing I knew, I had a name. I prayed for that person. Then I asked for another name. He gave me another individual. I continued until I drifted off again. I know it sounds silly, but I was surprised that each time I was given a name. Sometimes the name was a family member. Other times it was a friend whom I had not thought of in a while. I felt accomplished that night because I took just one more step of faith as I prayed for each person. I am hoping that these ideas will help those who share my sleepless nights. Whom can you pray for tonight when you wake?

Romans 8:1

"Therefore, there is now no condemnation for those who are in Christ Jesus."

Numbers

Our business hit a record year in 2019. God gave me a number that year. Numbers tend to stick in my head, and He knew it, so I was given "the number." The number was to be our sales number for the year. I was so afraid of that number that I didn't share it with my husband at first. It was so much more than we had ever made in previous years. I thought, *That is a good goal, for the future. But not attainable for 2019.* I would hold it close to my chest for a time. The number kept coming up every time I did the books each month. When I finally shared it with my husband, he responded positively and said it was up to God. Someone important once said that if your dreams do not scare you at times, maybe they are not big enough. Well, God gave me a big dream. I just had to accept it and step aside and watch Him do what He does best. As each month passed, I reviewed the books and shook my head in disbelief. We had changed multiple processes since I had started working with the company. However, those process changes did not equate to the amount of revenue the business was receiving. The calls were coming in like a flood.

My ego had got a bit in the way the previous year, because I had refused to hire someone to assist in the office. I did not need help. The business was not so big that I couldn't do all the work. Well, God had other plans. My husband had said when I started that we would grow large enough for me to need assistance. My mustard seed of faith said okay, but honestly, I did not see his vision. God had given my husband the vision. He gave me the numbers.

I finally cried uncle when the low-hanging fruit of paperwork stacked up on the desk. Hiring a friend to help was the best thing that happened to me. God used her to give me the space to breathe and tackle the phones and push through all the financials as the year progressed. He had set the plan in motion the year before and opened the doors during the current year, so we could be blessed as a company.

When the year was completed and all the books were reconciled, we passed the number He had given me. I was reminded of the number again. I could not imagine reaching that high. He knew we would surpass it, with His help. My mustard seed of faith kept the number hidden in my heart. He proved to me once again that He is the God of the hills and the valleys. All praises go to Him! Has God shown you a number, or a verse? Cling to that until He shows you His direction.

Luke 17:6

"He replied, 'If you have faith as small as a mustard seed, you can say to this mulberry tree, "Be uprooted and planted in the sea," and it will obey you.'"

2020

Be Still

When I woke up on January 1, 2020, I felt very excited to see where we would be at the end of the year. I had so many plans! My excitement was like Christmas Eve, staring at the presents under the twinkling tree. I could not wait for everyone to open what I got them the next morning.

My husband and I had plans to finally get away during the year. Over the years we had decided that experiences were more important than gifts. As a result, we had scheduled a few trips to experience life while we could. We had vacations planned and UME events in the schedule. The year was packed full of exciting ideas, and I could not wait for the trips to arrive. The anticipation was propelling me past the cold frost outside.

As I mentioned earlier, our business had hit a record year in 2019. God had blessed our business and opened new opportunities that we did not expect. We spent hours planning for 2020 business goals. We could see another record in the making, God willing. Monthly changes in processes and procedures had been our mantra for the last few years. We were starting to see the results of His favor. I felt determined to do our best as a company and see where God led us by the end of the year.

Little did I know that 2020 was not going to be the party I had expected, but more a test of my faith—along with everyone else across the world.

We were out of town when the stay-at-home mandate came out. Two weeks, we were told. Things would be back to normal in no time. As the adage goes, the writing on the wall spoke a different story. There was no way the government was going to send out checks to the American population for a two-week sabbatical.

We made jokes as the country slowly shut down, state by state. This can't last forever, right? I knew that a sense of humor was going to be required to get through this. I also knew that prayer was going to be my rock. We reached out to as many people as we could to reassure them that things would be back to normal fairly soon. However, our words seemed hollow in our heads as each day passed.

Slowly, as the weeks turned into months, casual optimism and humor turned into battle cries as we tried to keep some sense of normal. Masks and hand sanitizer were the new norm. Everyone asked what had happened to the toilet paper.

The business came to a screeching halt. We were receiving three calls a week. I jokingly told everyone that it was getting a bit desperate financially, so one of us may have to work at the local burger joint—and it would most likely be my husband, because he is cuter. I spent hours on my knees praying for guidance as we applied for any assistance we could receive.

All of the plans we had made to travel also came to a screeching halt. We were picking up the pieces, recouping our miles we had used for the trips. Everything was pushed slowly to the next year. And we weren't sure if the next year was even going to be viable.

Then one morning, I hit the wall. I was heading to the store to pick up the groceries for the month. My chest hurt and my anxiety was on overload. Wearing a mask in stores was hindering my breathing, which added to my stress. I heard a song on the radio and sat in the car for a Moment. Lauren Daigle sang, "Peace Be Still." The words washed over me, and I felt the Holy Spirit give me the peace I needed for the first time in a while. Reading scripture and living it are two totally different things. I needed the Spirit to give me strength. "Be still," I was told. I sat and listened quietly. Be still. I will fight for you. I put my mask on and downloaded the song to my phone. I walked into the store with my headset playing the song on repeat. I can't say that all of my stress went away. However, I felt the presence of the Spirit as I walked through the store. He didn't take it away, but He walked with me through it. That is what I needed.

Throughout the year, Holy Echoes of "Be still" came to me. Small ones at first, like the song in the car. Then louder, through everything I read. Everything I heard on the radio. This was a time to listen and not act. I am a person of action when under stress. This was new to me. There was nothing I could do but "Be still." Yet, it was enough. It still is enough. Holy Echoes...

Exodus 14:14

"The Lord will fight for you; you need only to be still."

Ecclesiastes 3

After my mom was saved, one of her favorite things to say was, "This is just a season." Everything had a season from Mom's viewpoint. God had shown her in many ways during her walk with Him that nothing is permanent; only He is. Mom clung to those words and shared them in good times and bad. She would paraphrase Ecclesiastes 3 to comfort me, and herself, during bad times. This meant that no matter how frustrating things might have felt, they were only for a season and eventually would end. The proverbial light-at-the-end-of-the-tunnel or rainbow-after-a-storm mentality. Mom liked to see past the pain to the promise.

Good or bad, we are all living "seasons" in our lives. Some we wish would stay forever, like a lingering kiss, a beautiful sunset, or a grand vacation with family. Others are not so pleasant: a broken promise, a lost job, or a loved one who has gone to be with the Lord... All are seasons, and all are temporary in life. The only solid, unchanging rock we have is God.

So why do I bring this scripture to you? Because COVID-19 is for a season. Yes, it will eventually be over and a forgotten, frustrating memory. It is still a season in our lives and a small speck in time of eternity.

Ecclesiastes 3:11

"He has made everything beautiful in its time. He has also set eternity in the human heart; yet so that no one can fathom what God has done from beginning to end."

Selling a House during COVID-19

The last thing on my mind during a pandemic was to sell my first home I had purchased. I had so many things that were screaming for my attention. The business was consuming my time. I had disaster loans to obtain and bills to negotiate with creditors as the calls slowed down to a halt. The last thing I wanted to do was add another large project to my plate.

However, God once again had other plans. My original goal was to keep the house after my husband and I were married for a future investment, and for our kids to rent in the meantime. Renting to family is another story for another time. Suffice it to say, we needed to sell the house with all the uncertainty in the business and the world. We were up against a wall, and I felt a bit uncomfortable facing that decision.

I had many internal battles over selling my little home. Wrapping my head around selling the first house I had purchased on my own was one struggle. I had worked so hard to get out of debt and purchase that house. Another struggle was that mom's remaining items were in the house, along with the grandfather clock that we didn't know where to keep. I didn't have the strength to decide what to do with all of her remaining valuables.

My final struggle, which was the biggest, was that my home happened to be the last piece of personal independence, and God knew it. I judged that I was totally committed to my husband and our lives together. However, this house was my "break the glass in case of emergency" ticket. When my husband and I met, I made more money than him, and he had been struggling with old debt from his marriage and child support. My little house was the "just in case" plan if he couldn't keep his home. It was also my "just in case" plan if... Having the home as a safety net was my security through our beginning years together. God wanted me to face all my internal struggles and trust Him alone. There is a part of the song "Burn the Ships" from the artists For King and Country that says:

"Burn the ships, cut the ties

Send a flare into the night

Say a prayer, turn the tide

Dry your tears and wave goodbye. "

I needed to "burn the ship" and cut that tie and trust God. My heart was open to His plans. My stomach was struggling like a seasick dog. I have spent many years of my life saying that I trust God in my journey. He calls me to the carpet on my spoken words of trust and asks me to place my feet where I spoke those words. Honestly, it is a journey that will take my entire life to accomplish.

The next six months would help my healing and cauterize the wounds so I could move forward. Steps of faith were made as we invested time and money in the home to get it ready for the new owners. My husband and I would spend every day after work and every weekend at the house for many weeks. I took photos and uploaded them to Facebook as I shared my journey of letting go. This journey became a blessing to me and to others that read my story. Each time I uploaded new photos, I saw the progress of healing, and I began to pray harder for the new owners. I wanted them to be as blessed as I was to find this home.

I am not going to say that it was a blissful journey. Selling a home is never an effortless and quick transaction. There were many stumbling blocks in the process. We had multiple items to repair and replace throughout the house. There were several loud discussions with my husband as we both became weary through the process. It didn't help that both of us were "Type A" personalities and perfectionists. We wanted the home perfect for the new owners and didn't leave a stone, or outlet, unturned. I knew we were heading down the rabbit hole one night when I was outside hosing the driveway down from dirt and my husband was vacuuming the crawl space no one would ever see. I laughed at the moment, but I kept hosing the driveway. Yes, that is the epitome of an OCD person.

The day I realized that we were heading to the final stages of putting the house on the market, I felt a huge sigh of relief. The previous anxious feelings of giving up the home had turned to feelings of inspiration and peace that He was in control of the process. We were deep into COVID at that time, and houses were selling like hotcakes on a Sunday afternoon. The home sold in a week. I craved to speak to the new owners but never had the opportunity. I prayed over the tree we had planted for Mom and prayed that the new owners would experience the blessings I had when they moved in.

Months later, through another God event, I was able to meet the new owner on Facebook. She shared with me how the house had been a blessing to her and was so delighted over all the work we had done. I was finally able to share with her how we had been praying for the new owners in the process, and though I had only received one offer, it was the one God wanted in our home. We still keep in touch, and she sends me pictures of Mom's tree. God also gave me a new friend during this entire process. She was our realtor for the sale of the home. God brought her to me during this time for encouragement and humor. I am so blessed to have her as a close friend today.

God is good. All the time. Trust the process and in faith, step forward when He calls you. Can you hear Him calling?

Proverbs 3:5

"Trust in the Lord with all your heart and lean not on your own understanding."

Psalm 56:3

"When I am afraid, I put my trust in you."

Romans 8:28

"And we know that in all things God works for the good of those who love him, who have been called according to his purpose."

The Grandfather Clock

My mother was very diligent in keeping things in safe places. She had a small safe for important papers. She had a place for everything. As she got older, finding those safe places became a treasure hunt. This story is about one of those hunts.

Mom acquired a beautiful grandfather clock that had been passed down from my grandparents. The clock itself wasn't unique. It was your average grandfather clock in appearance. But I loved this clock. I loved hearing the chimes when I visited their home. It had a soft, melodic sound that reassured me when I visited. It wasn't just a keeper of time, but a reminder of the memories each time I visited. I loved listening to the grandfather clock, and over the years enjoyed it again in my mother's home.

When we moved Mom from her home in Florida, I made the executive decision that we were hiring movers. It was easier for both of us and took a lot of stress off of her, as she wanted to make sure everything was in its safe place. The grandfather clock was no exception. The weights and pendulum had to be removed, carefully wrapped, and boxed away. The clock was officially locked when the movers arrived. Mom took the key and put it away in one of her safe places. The clock was wrapped with care and placed in the large moving van. We wished it well and knew we would see it soon.

When the van arrived at our New York home, we blessed the movers with two delivery locations for the furniture. I am certain they didn't agree with the "blessed" part. There was not enough room in my townhouse for it all, so most of the furniture was directed to a safe, climate-controlled storage space. The furniture stayed in that storage space until I purchased our new home one year later.

When the furniture was recovered from the storage space and delivered to our new home, the grandfather clock was revealed like a long-lost friend, tucked away. I was so excited to hear the music chimes again—like a kid at Christmas, waiting to open all the gifts. The movers uncovered the clock and carefully set it at the top of the stairs for us. I asked Mom where the boxes were located that had the weights, the pendulum, and the key.

We searched through the house in the mass of boxes and finally came upon one that had the weights and the pendulum. She reminded me that the key was in a different safe place and proceeded to look for it. We looked all over for that key. To save time, I will tell you that it was never found. She swears it was in the safe, or maybe with the clock, or maybe... The clock stood at the top of the stairs, almost speaking to the two of us: "I can't do this without you." Then it was mocking us in my head: "Here I stand, without a voice." I spent some time researching how to get a new key, to no avail. After the years went by, it just stood quietly as a reminder of what used to be.

As the grandfather clock stood at the top of the stairs, I would occasionally pass by and give it a longing glance. However, most days I didn't see it anymore, because I was so busy with the daily grind. When Mom passed, we kept the clock in that house while our kids rented. It was easier to have it there, and I wasn't sure what to do with it at the time. It was one more decision I didn't have the energy to make. Once the house was sold, I was forced to make that decision. My husband lovingly wrapped the clock once again, and it began the trip down the road to its new home. We placed it in a room off of the living room. It silently stood there, majestically overlooking the room.

After the other house was cleaned and sold, I decided to look for a key once again. I went online and found a local grandfather clock repair place. I called immediately and had the most delightful conversation with a person on the other end who was truly knowledgeable about these clocks. I didn't even know if he could get the clock running again—and by the way, we didn't have a key. The kind person on the other end of the phone said he would give it a try and scheduled a time to come over. When he arrived, I had the weights and the pendulum, but no stick and no key. The weights were wrapped in a newspaper. When I unwrapped them, I discovered that the paper was dated the day we had moved Mom out. Hope rose inside me as I carefully cut out the date in the paper.

The repairman brought in his tools and with the skills of a surgeon, started taking the clock apart from the back. He then gingerly took the mechanism and placed it in a handmade carrier. He said he would take it back to his shop and see what he could do.

After a week or so I got a friendly call from the Clock Doc, and he said we were good to go. He brought back my mechanism, and in the same gentle way, put the grandfather clock back together. He had found a key to fit the door as well. I was more than excited. It was a quick process at that point, and the next thing I knew, the clock was playing his chimes once again after so many years.

It was like my grandparents were back in that room, sharing the unbelievable joy I felt. Then quickly, the joy turned to frustration toward me. Why hadn't I thought of this before? I had waited so long, and I could have fixed this years ago. I felt God quietly speak to me: "There is a time for everything." It was time for the clock to come to life once again. With all I had been dealing with during the past year and selling the house, this clock brought clarity to my soul. Everything happens in His time, not mine. Another lesson of who is in control. I needed that. Listening to the clock chime every day reminds me of time, and His timing. What timing are you hearing today?

Ecclesiastes 3:6-7

"A time to search and a time to give up, a time to keep and a time to throw away, a time to tear and a time to mend, a time to be silent and a time to speak."

Toothbrush Story

My husband decided that we needed new electric tooth-brushes. Sometimes it is more cost-effective than buying the brush heads separately–akin to buying a new razor to save money on blades. I must admit, I was excited. You know you are getting old when a new toothbrush makes your day. Can you relate? Not to the old part, but new household items. It is funny how they bring joy to the craziness of our days.

One morning I was brushing my teeth with my new fancy toothbrush, and I noticed that it would stop, and then suddenly start again. I stopped brushing and thought about it for a bit. Had this happened before? I vaguely remembered that it had. I was so busy with the morning routine that I really didn't notice it at first. The more I thought about it, the more I had to know why. I knew that most electric toothbrushes had a timer on them so I could brush non-stop until it stopped after two minutes. I felt amused by that bonus. We have been told by the "experts" that we need to brush for two minutes. How do I know how long two minutes are? A song in my head? Counting to 120? This invention made my day. Two minutes completed when the toothbrush stopped. However, what was causing it to stop and start again?

I started brushing my teeth again and noticed that the tooth-brush did this process over and over. I started down the rabbit hole of wondering why. I purposely started the process over to see how many times it did this. Yes, I actually did that. Three times the toothbrush turned off and then restarted until the two minutes were completed. Why three times? Then after timing it–yes, I did that too–I realized that the brush stopped after thirty seconds and then restarted. After a few minutes of internal calculations, I realized that if you divided your mouth into four sections, you would be able to spend thirty seconds on each section and complete the process in two minutes. Wow, how cool was that? Honestly, I am not sure if someone did according to my hypothesis, but it did seem sound. I was happy and then went along with my routine.

I had to share it with my husband. The next time we were doing our morning routine, I stopped and shared with him my new revelation. He looked at me and smiled a bit. Good thing he understands me. I asked him if he had noticed that it was occurring with his toothbrush. He said that he had kind of noticed, but didn't think any more about it. He said he just "brushed it off," so to speak, and kept brushing his teeth. I was so excited with my new revelation and couldn't see why he wasn't as excited.

This was my teachable moment from God. God gently reminded me that He had created my husband and me different for a reason. I think about the tiniest details daily. That is what makes me a good finance and project manager. He can see a toothbrush and never think about it again unless it doesn't work properly. Then he will fix it. He didn't see that small detail as a problem. So, he compartmentalized it and moved on. We are made different on purpose. We complement each other with our differences. If we were both the same, one of us would not be needed. How cool is God to bring us together with our differences and show me why they need to exist? What relationships are struggling in your life because of simple differences? Ask God to show you the blessings in the differences.

1 Corinthians 12:18-20

"But in fact God has placed the parts in the body, every one of them, just as he wanted them to be. If they were all one part, where would the body be? As it is, there are many parts, but one body."

I Am the Vine

The scriptures from John 15:1-8 about the vine and the branches have spoken to me over and over in my years as a Christian. When I was first saved, it was my mantra. I knew if I didn't plug into Him and read His Word that I was going to miss His messages to me. I was a new bud on the branch, drinking the nutrients of His Word and His love. I was strengthened daily as I walked with Him and learned through scripture what His plans were for me. I loved that time. I naïvely thought that the feelings would never go away. What I didn't realize is that our walk is not always about great feelings. They can be deceptive. For example, when you are first married, there is that honeymoon glow everyone talks about. I know I've felt it. You judge that you will always be happy and never fight. Yes, I was a bit naïve during my first marriage. A marriage gets stronger when the difficulties arise. Like a tree rooted deeply into the ground. If the tree has deep roots, it can withstand the storms. If I am deeply rooted in God, I can withstand life's storms. Clinging to the vine kept me fed, spiritually and mentally.

When I stepped away from my walk with Him, I was again drawn to the images of the vine. Quietly, He whispered, "Come back to me." He was reminding me that without Him, I was going to die spiritually. He gives me life when I stay connected to Him. I felt cold and alone when I walked away. He reminded me that my life was in Him and not on my own. Like a cut flower, it eventually dies, because all the nutrients are in the roots and soil. I was that cut flower that looked good on the outside at first, and then began to shrivel from the inside. My spirit was missing the closeness I'd had.

During 2020 and COVID, the vine images were everywhere. He reminded me that He would never let me go. I knew that if I didn't cling to him during the pandemic, fear might take over, and I would start doing things in my own strength again. I clung to him like our puppy Benny clings to Dad during a thunderstorm. I knew that He was my sustenance and my peace. Reading John 15 gave me the peace and hope I needed as we struggled through the pandemic. The business fluctuated like a tossing boat in a storm. He reminded me daily that if we held on to Him, we were going to make it as a family and a business when the storm was over.

It was not all love and flowers as we clung to Him. There was a bit of pruning during the time of COVID. Sometimes God uses circumstances to prune us and in turn make us stronger. We have a peach tree. That tree rarely gives us fruit. Some years we seriously think about just removing the tree because the leaves are sparse, and the fruit is in short supply. However, when we prune the tree back drastically, we see the leaves once again come to life the next year. The fruit may not be much, but give it a few years and you start to see results. God does this with us as well.

Going through COVID, I was pruned by change. I *hate* change. As mentioned previously, I am obsessive-compulsive and a "Type A" personality. I like change as much as I like riding a roller coaster with motion sickness. I am green with the first turn on the ride. I hated quarantine, masks, finding toilet paper, new business requirements, "new normal," and changes in our United Marriage Encounter ministry. I could go on, but you get the picture. I wanted everything back to the way it was. I struggled between disappointment and panic. Disappointment over missed trips we had planned for a year. Panic over finding food and essentials while avoiding people. What a year of change. God used 2020 to show me that I can make it through all changes if I hold on to Him and cling to His truths. I am so grateful for His faithfulness and the continuous reminders through His Word. Pruning is still not easy. But if we focus on the end result of His perfection, we can make it through. Cling today to the Vine. Resist the urge to pull back when He prunes. He only does it in love.

John 15:1-8

"I am the true vine, and my Father is the gardener. He cuts off every branch in me that bears no fruit, while every branch that does bear fruit he prunes so that it will be even more fruitful. You are already clean because of the word I have spoken to you. Remain in me, as I also remain in you. No branch can bear fruit by itself; it must remain in the vine. Neither can you bear fruit unless you remain in me.

"I am the vine; you are the branches. If you remain in me and I in you, you will bear much fruit; apart from me you can do nothing. If you do not remain in me, you are like a branch that is thrown away and withers; such branches are picked up, thrown into the fire and burned. If you remain in me and

my words remain in you, ask whatever you wish, and it will be done for you. This is to my Father's glory, that you bear much fruit, showing yourselves to be my disciples."

9-Volt Battery

We purchased a safe for the house. We wanted one for valuables and to keep the guns safely together. When we went to the store, they gave us two lock options. We could have a digital or a manual lock. I had not thought about having options and was intrigued with the concept. The manual locks looked cool, but ominous, with the large boat-like steering wheel to open the safe. I suddenly thought of the pirate days of old. This could be fun, right? I then looked at the digital locks, which were more subdued, with a quick code to punch in for a speedy entry. We finally decided that the safe with the digital lock was the one we wanted. It was easier and gave us the option to reprogram the code when needed. We brought home the safe, set it up, and programmed the lock with a new code. What fun that was, trying to find a code both my husband and I would remember no matter what. But I digress. We filled the safe and closed the door to lock everything in. I was content with our decision, knowing we had one more project completed from our never-ending list.

Things went great for quite a while. I would either secure something in the safe or occasionally retrieve an item or two we might need. One sunny day, I went to our safe to get something and punched in the familiar code. Nothing. I punched in the code again. Nothing again. Slight panic started to rise within me. I slowly but deliberately punched in the code a third time. I thought maybe I was being too hasty and needed to slow down to not miss a number. I was wrong. After a few more attempts, I re-alized I was acting out the true definition of insanity. I was doing the same thing again and again, expecting different results. The black safe stood, silently mocking me, as I grew more anxious. I walked away and dug out the manual in my desk to see what I was doing wrong or what needed to be fixed. As I scanned the manual, I found the section needed to help me with my dilemma. I needed a battery. Not just any battery, but a 9-volt battery. Cool, I had one of those. I was excited to find such an easy solution.

I walked into the kitchen and found the battery I needed. I brought the battery back to the safe, and after a few attempts, I opened the lock mechanism and changed the battery. I punched in the code and was so excited, like playing the slots, when the safe magically opened. God is good! I went on my merry way, excited to share the news with my husband. I could fix things!

My new shiny pride was only for a moment, though. A few days later I went to the familiar safe and punched in the code. Nothing. Seriously? I punched in the code again and had the same result—nothing. I started to feel like the movie *Groundhog Day*. If you have seen this movie, you will understand. If you haven't, you must see that movie, and it will explain my feelings to a tee. I went back to the kitchen in frustration, stating to myself that I did not have time for this. I grabbed another battery from the drawer and stomped back to the mocking safe. I put another new battery in the safe and punched in the code. Nothing. Seriously?

I went back to the manual in my desk and flipped pages until I found the 1-800-help-me-the-heck-out number. I called and sat on hold for quite a while. When the happy representative answered, I proceeded to share my dilemma. She asked if I had changed the battery. Of course I had. I wouldn't have called if I hadn't checked everything first. I had to step back a moment. I was so frustrated, I forgot that they probably deal with customers who are not as savvy as I was with my manual reading skills. I took a breath and we walked through all the steps again.

She then asked me if I had installed a particular brand of 9-volt battery. Excuse me? A battery is a battery, right? I was corrected and told that in the manual, it specifically mentions that a particular 9-volt battery needs to be used. I had seen that in the manual, but had assumed that a battery was a battery. What company wants you to use a specific brand of battery? It made no sense. Well, in reality she was right, because it stated it in the manual, and they'd had this issue previously with other customers. After changing the battery one more time, with the correct brand, I was able to open the safe once more.

After contemplating my day, I realized there were two lessons for me from this story. First, to always know the code. If I had not memorized the code, I would not have been able to obtain the treasures in my safe. Also, the code to life is Him, and His Word. Without God and His Word, we are unable to open the treasures that He offers.

My second lesson was to follow the instruction manual to the letter. One small deviation from the instructions can send me off course. One degree of difference can change the entire course of a ship. I had blindly assumed that the battery was the same, when in fact it was not. I had missed one very important part of the manual. I thought I knew it all. Once again, God demonstrated to me that I should stop relying on my own strength and reach out to Him. I need to stay in His Word and not deviate from His instructions to keep me from falling off course. Remember to memorize the code and follow His instructions.

John 14:6

"Jesus answered, 'I am the way and the truth and the life. No one comes to the Father except through me.'"

Willow Trees

Willows have a special place in my heart. I look at many plants and trees and see God's beauty, and often I am reminded of a scripture. When I see a willow tree, I am reminded of the Israelites hanging their harps on the willow trees and weeping while in Babylon. They struggled horribly in captivity when they walked away from their Father and His path for them. I am reminded of how easy it is to stray like the Israelites, and how we are able to cry out to God in our struggles. I am grateful for His constant mercy and grace as we come back to Him after straying.

I purchased a willow tree for the front of our property as a reminder. If you know anything about willow trees, they grow like weeds. I had a few willow trees at my first home and used them as a natural fence from the neighbors behind us. I love the fact they can be beautiful to view and a barrier to the world around us. The willow we purchased grew into a large, billowing tree before we knew it. Another thing about willow trees is that maintenance and pruning is necessary, unless you are planning on keeping it in a wooded area by itself. Trimming our willow has become an annual event and important, as it grows bigger each year. It is therapeutic being outside, and I enjoy the pruning process.

While pruning our willow one sunny afternoon, I was given a few reminders by God. I carefully pruned back each branch until it was above my head, to give the mower a chance to go underneath to cut the grass below. As I started the process, I noticed the branches were touching the ground. The poor tree was burdened by the weight of the branches. God stepped in and reminded me that I let things burden me down sometimes when I should be giving them to Him. As the willow was burdened by her branches, they dragged her to the ground. How many times have I carried burdens that were not mine to carry? I only needed to give them to Him, and he would give me the rest I needed.

The second reminder given to me was about pruning. Pruning is needed for plants and trees but is not always pretty or fun during the process. Pruning is needed for me as well. My Father in heaven shared again that the pruning process was to make me more like Him. Pruning is a bit messy at times, and I can blame the shears instead of focusing on the end results. Pruning the willow takes time and patience for the one holding the shears. You want to make sure that the branches are pruned correctly and not just ripped from the tree. Careful pruning gives the tree life. Careful pruning in my life gives me new growth and perspective. I need to trust the process. The end results of pruning are spectacular, and He deserves all the credit.

There is always a cleanup period after pruning. Cleaning up all the branches can be messy and time-consuming. It doesn't happen instantly. It is the same with my life. When God prunes things out of my life, I often want to hide from the world and "look" perfect externally. He says, "No, show everyone where you came from and the process, so you can be a help to others going through the same process." I need to show scars and all, so I can help others in their journey. I spent so many years hiding His methods because I was afraid. We all need reminders of the mess, to show others they can get through their mess as well. It takes time and it takes the family of God. We can't clean up our messes alone. We need each other.

In the end, after pruning and cleaning up, there are a few

remnants of the branches or leaves lying on the ground. They are reminders of what happened. They are also to remind me that I am not perfect, and of what He did for me. Isn't God amazing, how He speaks to us while we are doing our daily activities? God speaks in the quiet of the day through the nature around us. Step outside today and take time to listen to Him. What is He sharing with your heart?

Psalm 137:2 (AMP)

"On the willow trees in the midst of Babylon we hung our harps."

Matthew 11:28

"Come to me, all you who are weary and burdened, and I will give you rest."

Mending Fences

No one expected COVID-19 to have such an impact on their lives. The entire world was impacted. It was like September 11, but with a global effect. No one was safe from this invisible disease. It impacted every age, race, economic class, and country. My husband and I watched the news as states completely shut down, one by one. People were isolated and scared. With modern transportation slowing down to a halt, work and families were forced into online communication. Businesses suffered financially, till many had to close. Everyone missed personal connections, and hugs became a thing of the past. It was an end-of-the-world experience, where no cure was in sight.

Who could have seen this massive wave of isolation take place in this century? Well, God knew it was coming and was not surprised by COVID. Nothing surprises God. We should have reassurance, knowing that He knew it was coming and knows when it will end. We should also have peace, knowing that He is in control and on the throne, no matter what happens to us. As Christians, we can cling to that statement. We know how the book ends. We can stand in the knowledge that our days are numbered and will not end one minute before our time on this earth is complete. That knowledge kept my fears at bay during 2020. I shared that information with everyone I spoke to through social media and by phone. The world needed hope. The world needed Jesus.

As the country shut down, I had a driving desire to share that hope with everyone. God was speaking to my heart once again. This was the best time to share the Gospel of Christ! We could reach out to everyone we knew! People everywhere were looking for an answer to their fears. Christ is always the answer. What better time to reach those hurting than 2020? Grudges between friends and family were softened by quarantine. People were receptive to hearing the truth. I used that time to reach out to them.

Our little family was not protected from internal drama. There have been disagreements and misunderstandings through the years. Some with our kids, and some with extended family. My husband and I used the time of softened hearts to reach out to everyone in our family. This was our opportunity to share God's love and peace with them. Some were receptive, and some were not. When my husband was first saved, a few of his family believed I had ushered him into a cult. They didn't understand that God had reached Carl, and that I was just the vessel to speak truth into his heart.

Isn't it cool how God accepts us where we are and then begins the slow process of change in us to become more like Him? My husband has changed over the years, and they saw a different person from the one they once knew. He was transforming into the man that God had called him to be. That change affected their view of him. I understood the conflict. I went through the same murmurings when I became a Christian. People who knew me before wondered if I was either pretending to be something I was not, or worse, looking down on them for their actions. Over the years, I have concluded that it is up to God to soften their hearts toward me, and my job is to lean into Him as He works on me. I can only control my actions and walk. It is not our job to fix anyone. We can only pray and stay consistent in our walk. We are not perfect, just forgiven.

We are still praying for the restoration of our entire family. God does not want us to be separate, but to lift each other up in His love. I believe in miracles and pray for each family member by name. We will not stop praying for the miracle. We have not stopped sharing with our family and friends. It is in His timing, and I am waiting expectantly for His work in our family. What family member can you pray for today?

John 16:33

"I have told you these things, so that in me you may have peace. In this world you will have trouble. But take heart! I have overcome the world."

Ephesians 6:15

"And with your feet fitted with the readiness that comes from the gospel of peace."

Patience & Slowing Down

More than any other year, the Lord used 2020 to teach me patience. I am not a patient person and spend most of my time trying to get tasks or projects completed *before* the deadline. Growing up in the military, we were taught that being on time was considered late and being early was considered on time. I framed my life and actions around those concepts. Waiting or being patient during a process is not a part of my DNA. I habitually find tasks I can add to my daily routine so I can shorten my mental to-do list. This process tends to increase the impatience within me, because I leave no extra time for the unexpected things that come up.

Then 2020 came and caught me by surprise. My husband and I had so many plans and activities to accomplish. The year 2020 and COVID-19 did not care about my plans or my impatience. Our business, United Marriage Encounter, and my daily life were rocked by COVID-19. I had to learn the concept that having patience does not mean I am lazy. It is waiting on His will for something and not my own. Patience is waiting on God and not plowing through in my own strength. I needed to let my heavenly Father guide me in His time, not mine. Notice I said the same thing three different ways? I often need to hear things multiple times before it sinks in. If I try to control my situation, I am stating that I know more than God does about my circumstances. It sounds ridiculous at first, but how many times do we do that without realizing it?

Patience can bring clarity and vision as we sit and wait for a direction from God. Patience sometimes means staying quiet and waiting for time to pass, or for a person to work through a solution. Patience takes practice. Patience means I need to slow down. I can be a bull in a China shop, pleading my case instead of allowing them to come to a conclusion in their own time. When COVID hit, I saw the writing on the wall with the business. We had to act fast so that the business would not fail. I acted quickly to obtain the loans and assistance needed to keep us afloat. Those quick actions helped us through the rest of the year financially. Patience was not needed there, except for when using the websites that were overloaded with requests. The small business association website crashed on and off for days as I pushed through to get the loans we needed. I wasn't patient, but I was persistent and successfully won the fight at the end of the day. I work well with those types of challenges.

However, using the same methods in our marriage ministry and personal plans was not as effective. I needed to be patient. I wanted everything to stay the same in the ministry, without any changes from COVID. I impatiently voiced my opinion and did not consider others as they worked through the same process. I wanted everything back to the way it was before COVID. Again, issues with change. My impatience got in the way, and God stepped in.

Quietly, I heard Him speak to my spirit: "Who are you to think you know better than God?" That stopped me for a minute. Was I attempting to "fix" things that He had allowed or planned? Did I think I could make better decisions? I would never verbally state that I was smarter than God. But was I doing it by my hasty actions? This was a humbling moment for me. I needed to slow down and let His process take place in my life. This is an ongoing practice for me. I am not "there" yet and won't be "there" until I am face-to-face with my Savior. I was told by someone important that God often allows us to step out on our own without intervening as a lesson to grow. He will coax us along in our lesson so that we grow in our management of lifetime situations. I needed to learn a lesson. Thank you, Lord, for 2020, which showed me my shortcoming of impatience. Pray today to be open to our heavenly Father, who can not only reveal shortcomings, but give you the strength to work through them.

Colossians 3:12

"Therefore, as God's chosen people, holy and dearly loved, clothe yourselves with compassion, kindness, humility, gentleness and patience."

Proverbs 25:15

"Through patience a ruler can be persuaded, and a gentle tongue can break a bone."

Christmas 2020

Listening to "It's the Most Wonderful Time of the Year," I laughed to myself because it was Christmas 2020. I judged everything I that thought Christmas should be that day. In my head, Christmas should be a time for family and friends gathering around meals. Laughter, presents, and breaking bread together were on the top of my list.

I understand the meaning of Christmas and appreciate church every year as we get closer to the birthday of Christ. I get excited each year as I decorate and place manger scenes all over the house to remind myself what the true meaning of Christmas is. I love to make the house "Christmas," with decorations everywhere. There is no safe space. You can often go into one of the bathrooms and find a decoration or two. My grandmother used to do the same thing, and I want to continue the tradition.

However, each year I may occasionally get carried away purchasing gifts for everyone. Okay, more than occasionally. Okay, fine—every year I get a bit carried away. This is because I feel so blessed by what God has done for us that I want to give back to everyone and share His blessings. I love to watch the face of the unsuspecting person when I can fill their cup through an action or a gift.

I start planning Christmas around September on my spreadsheet. Yes, I use a spreadsheet. Do not laugh; some people who are reading this will totally understand my OCD nature. Others will appreciate my attentiveness to getting things done in order. I create a budget each year, and it is easier to save a little each month during the year instead of blowing said budget in December. Then I begin the journey of prayer and the hunt. I pray about what to give each person and search online, mostly, to obtain the goods. As each month goes by, I check off my spreadsheet and push hard not to go over my budget.

Then in mid-November, I start to ask everyone what they want for Christmas. Each family member gives me more suggestions to complete my task, not knowing I have already started the process so many months ago.

Most years, I stick to my allotted budget. Some years, things happen, and I blow the budget completely. One year in particular, my husband needed a tool cabinet for his business because the old one had to be returned to its previous owner. I had a little extra money in my savings, so I used it. I drove to Lowe's at the eleventh hour and asked for the biggest one they had in stock. It was huge! I had no idea what I was looking at because again, I know software and project management, not tools or equipment. I just knew that it had a ton of drawers and was bigger than me. I almost bought the one that had the built-in radio. But I did not.

Lowe's was kind enough to ship it directly, for a cost, the week after Christmas. I took a picture of the steel rolling tool cabinet and placed it in a box under the tree for my husband. Yes, I may have gotten a bit carried away that year. But the look on his face was priceless. I love to bless him and my family any time I can.

This year, in 2020, God had other plans. As I watched the snow melt and the temperatures rise on Christmas Eve in Upstate NY, I felt pushed to write His thoughts to me. The wind was blowing as the temps rose and seemed to beckon me to listen carefully what He was trying to tell me. Some of these stories here were those thoughts.

Christmas 2020 was filled with family sickness, estrangement, stress, and not what I wanted or expected for the season. My father-in-law had just had surgery and was back in the hospital. My mother-in-law was praying that she could bring him home for Christmas. As the days went by, it was looking more like a Christmas miracle if it occurred. A friend was also away from home and family, rehabbing a fractured hip. She was not going to be home for Christmas. Other family members were struggling with their health. One of our kids was estranged due to circumstances that were out of my control. Another was away and not able to come home due to COVID. The stress of it all was shrinking the Christmas spirit in my heart. I wanted to fix it all and have everyone together.

As I looked back and dove into my Bible, I started to get a new perspective of what Christmas is not. The first Christmas was not much different than 2020. There was an unplanned pregnancy, inconvenient and difficult travel plans, strife in government, and no room at the inn. If I had to plan that season, there would be helpers everywhere to assist as everyone came into town for the census. Homes would be opened and food available for as many people as possible. Pregnant women would not have to sleep in a barn, but in my bed if necessary. I am sure Joseph and Mary were walking completely by faith at that time. Nothing seemed to go as planned for them.

But God had designed it all. He had a plan. It was not supposed to be a parade or grandiose display to the world. Only to certain people–the shepherds and the Magi. There was a quietness and stillness that forced Joseph and Mary to focus on what was important. This event needed their full attention. No distractions from the world.

He also designed 2020. Nothing is a surprise to God. He spoke to me through the silent night and the quietness of the day. There was no hustling around to parties and visiting friends and family. Only the quiet moments with Him instead. He wants me to hear Him more. Something is coming. Just like over 2,000 years ago, something is in the air. Miracles are in process, and I need to be patient. Yes, I have presents under the tree and cookies on the counter. But they are not the focus this year. He is coming. The signs are in the air. We can celebrate together that the event over 2,000 years ago pointed to the next coming of Christ. Are you ready? Come, Lord Jesus, come.

Revelation 22:7

"Look, I am coming soon! Blessed is the one who keeps the words of the prophecy written in this scroll."

Purple Robes

Christmas time for my husband and me is a great opportunity to spend time together with our family and friends. The meaning of Christmas has grown for us over the years as we press closer to Christ. The year my husband accepted Christ, he saw new meaning during his first Christmas. That understanding has brought us closer together as a couple. I get more excited each Christmas, knowing it is more special to him. That is my most precious gift.

Christmas also gives us time to bless each other with an afternoon of shopping and wrapping. We are at an age where we don't "need" anything. What we do is set aside a day to have lunch and then go to the local mall and pick a couple of stores to shop together. This is a fun experience, because we pick out something for each other and then take our gifts home to wrap and place under the tree. We both know what we are getting, but the fun is in the adventure together at the mall. Sometimes it is clothes, or a unique item we find on sale. And sometimes it is an "aha" moment of one of us remembering a special gift the other had wanted. Those times are exciting, because they are few and far between. Again, the adventure together is the ultimate goal.

In 2020, Christmas was not like previous years, and our shopping together was cut short due to COVID and other important tasks that came up. Due to the time crunch, we decided to get each other something small online and not do our customary tradition. Online shopping became our friend during 2020. We could get just about anything with a click of a button. Sometimes I am not sure if it is a good or bad thing. The ease of clicking a button is not as painful as the old credit card machine that made the "rick rack" sound when you made a purchase. You had to think for a minute when you took the credit card out and watched them put the carbon paper over it before making the noise. You had time to reconsider a purchase.

In 2020 it was a different Christmas experience. Neither would know what the other had purchased. A new adventure! As Christmas got closer, I bought my husband's gifts and had them wrapped nicely under the tree. He also went shopping online and did the same. We were excited to see what each other had purchased. Christmas morning came quick, and after coffee, the two of us sat down to unwrap our gifts to each other.

I need to stop here and give a quick backstory. When I was younger, I had an experience with a family member who spray painted several visible items purple, and in turn some of the kids at school mocked me for it. I decided at that time that I hated purple. I wanted nothing to do with the color and avoided it when purchasing anything. God's sense of humor is such that when I got back to the United States many years later, the "in" color was purple. Seriously. You cannot make that up. I hated the color for the longest time. I know, "hate" is a strong emotion toward a color. However, at fifteen years of age, I hated purple. As I grew older, I still avoided the color in my wardrobe and in any decorations. I did not "hate" it like I did I was younger but tolerated it from a distance.

So, back to opening gifts. I opened one gift from my husband, and to my surprise there were two matching purple bathrobes. I laughed to myself over the irony, but I *loved* them so much, because they were not only soft and fluffy, but *matching*! We were going to be secret twins no one would know about.

Well, except now, you also know. As I sat with my new robe, I heard the Lord speak to me: "You are a chosen people, a royal priesthood" (1 Peter 2:9). Purple was considered a royal color during biblical times. This was a symbol that we were God's possession and that He had plans for us as a couple. I held the robe close and took in His message. Purple suddenly had a new meaning for me. I thanked God for the message and for the new meaning.

After the holiday ended and the dust settled, we did go back out and enjoyed our annual tradition at the local mall. However, I will always cherish my purple robe, remembering what God shared with me on Christmas 2020. His timing is always perfect. Never ignore small messages that may come in a color.

1 Peter 2:9

"But you are a chosen people, a royal priesthood, a holy nation, God's special possession, that you may declare the praises of him who called you out of darkness into his wonderful light."

Proverbs 31:22

"She makes coverings for her bed; she is clothed in fine linen and purple."

More God Moments

More Holy Echoes

Have you ever read a verse and it resonated with you? This is what happens to me on many occasions. Exodus 14:14, "*The Lord will fight for you; you need only to be still.*" Psalm 46:10, "*Be still, and know that I am God.*" I heard those verses over and over throughout 2020.

As 2021 came around, I still heard it in songs on the radio, on social media, and in my devotion time. Then it slowly changed, like seeing the buds on a tree and knowing that spring is around the corner. It was a quiet whisper at first. Like when you wake a sleeping child. "Get ready, again." I have heard those words before, but like a slow quiet drum roll that gets louder, the words "Get ready, again" spoke to me.

I thought I was ready. *What am I getting ready for now, Lord?* In reality, I had spent the past year hunkering down, trying to make sure we made it through the season, like a person huddled in a bomb shelter. There was so much that came about from 2020. We were trying to survive at the business. Then there was politics, COVID, riots, unrest, and those stupid masks... I was ready for a change. As I heard Him speak to me, "Get ready, again," I wondered what this new season would entail.

What I did not realize is that He was preparing my husband as well. As we prepared for the months ahead with daily jobs at our company, we both had been sidelined by work and had not spent as much time together in His Word as we should have. I sat and wrote one weekend to my husband. I heard the Lord speak to my heart that it was time to wake up from our slumber and get out of the bunker. Time to look beyond work again and start afresh. Change was coming, and we needed to get ready.

Another weekend soon after, I felt compelled to share with my husband that it was time for us to dig deeper individually and as a couple. When I shared this with him, he laughed and said that the Lord had been giving him gentle nudges to get back on track. So, we were in unison. But what were we preparing for?

My husband went to Godly counsel and asked for help to get "unstuck." God has a sense of humor, because he was told to get back into His Word, listen to his instincts (the Holy Spirit), and listen to his wife. I laughed because I was asking for the same help and was told to listen to what God was sharing with me and to trust my husband's instincts. Confirmation comes together as a couple reaches out for signs. Isn't it funny that when you are looking for a sign, He often gives it in many different ways to confirm and to repeat what He wants us to hear? Holy Echoes...

Jeremiah 1:17

"Get yourself ready! Stand up and say to them whatever I command you. Do not be terrified by them, or I will terrify you before them."

What Are We Preparing For?

What I have learned so far through life is that when God gives you a word, be ready for the attack that follows. I thought I knew what that meant. I was wrong. My husband and I went away on trips three weekends back-to-back. I was excited, but also hesitant to see what God was going to do. You know when something is coming, but you are kind of afraid to see what it is going to be? That is me...

The first weekend He met us at our hotel, and as my husband said he was stuck and had received what he was supposed to do, God also reached me and told me what I needed to do, like I mentioned earlier. I proceeded with baby steps and shared with the small group of couples the vision I saw of large angels standing behind them and hedging them in as we pressed on to help the new couples in their marriages. He was protecting us, and we just needed to lean in. There were more visions that weekend. He kept showing me tiny glimpses behind the curtain.

The second weekend He met us there again, and shared deeper. He told me that we needed to trust Him and start using what He had shared with us. I *loved* that bubble of worship and peace we experienced that weekend. It was a mountain top experience. I heard Him speak to me so loudly. I could share in boldness and without fear to my husband. He knew we were on the right path, and we were being called to go deeper. I sat at the hotel, just basking in His peace and love. There was so much love and clarity. I didn't want to leave that spot. It was like seeing the sun come up on the top of a mountain and not wanting to leave the site. I was afraid to leave that spot. I asked for a word from my heavenly Father, and it would come to me every morning. It was an awesome feeling of fellowship and love and grace.

The third weekend I felt God calling me to the next level. It was time, He was telling me. I asked for strength and started to share what I saw. "Wake up" came clearly before the alarm went off one morning. I shared those words with the couples in the conference room that day. The longer I was there that weekend, the braver I got, and I shared more of what He had told me. We were to get ready, and there was going to be a bigger battle for marriages and lives for Christ.

This was the turning point. I have reached it before with Him. But I have stepped back in fear of the attack. The enemy came in like a flood and destroyed what God had called me to do so many years ago. What was I going to do? I had two choices. Press in, or walk away. I took a deep breath and pressed in, and asked for His divine guidance that I wasn't doing any of this in my strength. The confirmations came in like a flood, and we walked away from the weekend with a stronger spirit and determination. I was so excited for the next steps.

Then it came. From the minute I got off the plane, after three weeks of listening to the Lord through the events we had attended, I was pushed against the wind in attacks from the enemy. At home, and at work. I thought it would be notified attacks.

I was so naïve. In reality, I didn't get off the plane from our third trip before the first attack. One of the airline stewards came at me like a flood. I was caught off guard at first. I thought he must have been having a bad day. It seemed small and bit frustrating at the time. God spoke to me after that attack and said, "I am going to give you the words to say, and your husband will be your protector." Like a soldier protecting the camp. I laughed, because I have always stood up for myself and didn't plan on needing someone else to "protect" me. I wasn't sure if I was ready for his help.

Then it grew bigger. It was like the enemy was taunting me and saying, "Do you really want to do this? Remember what happened last time? You are going to fail. They are not going to accept you. Your husband is going to fight you." I, again, didn't expect this attack. Who was I that anyone would find important enough to come against what I was sharing? I thought I could deal with this. I believed the small attacks I received daily could be fought with my shield from God. I didn't realize that my tiny shield needed work.

I also didn't expect the discouragement to come from my husband. After all, we had just spent three weekends on the mountain top. How could anything come between us? Again, naïve. I tried to use logic as we fought and shared with him that the enemy was just trying to get between us. It didn't work. We both have different love languages. His is acts of service. Mine is words of encouragement. I know how to bless him with in his love language as I run the business, make meals, and run the household. The enemy knows his weakness like he knows mine. As I tried to keep things in order at home and work, he let the enemy get between us and played old tapes in his head. So instead of words of encouragement, I was receiving words of discouragement.

So many words of discouragement that I wanted to just crawl

up in a ball and say, "Okay, okay, I give in." But deep in my spirit, I knew He was calling me to do His will, so I needed to put my big girl pants on and stand in His strength. I needed my armor more than ever before. It was time to get serious.

I immediately looked online for Bible plans to dig deeper, and for spiritual warfare. There were so many, and multiple scriptures to help me refocus. Also, before we left our last weekend away, I was given a book titled *Praying God's Word* by Beth Moore. I know that wasn't a coincidence, but a God moment that said, "Get ready and dig deeper. You are going to take this journey alone for a bit to cling to Me, and then there will be others to come alongside of you later. But for now, you will focus on Me and nothing else." I wanted nothing better than to reach out to others for help. You know, a person with arms to hug me and say, "It's going to be okay." I knew He was in control. I had to go back to scripture to confirm in my head where the enemy was trying to swim. I reached for my Bible and looked for that anchor. He met me there...

Psalm 91:1-2

"Whoever dwells in the shelter of the Most High will rest in the shadow of the Almighty. I will say of the Lord, 'He is my refuge and my fortress, my God, in whom I trust.'"

Psalm 9:9

"The Lord is a refuge for the oppressed, a stronghold in times of trouble."

Psalm 16:1

"Keep me safe, my God, for in you I take refuge."

Psalm 46:1

"God is our refuge and strength, an ever-present help in trouble."

I am not going to say that things suddenly changed here and all was well. On occasion, it does turn out like that. God does move mountains in an instant. He is the Great Provider and Healer! However, at other times, He takes us through the valleys to cling to Him more and stay focused. "Stay close to Me," he whispers in the dark. Remember, He has three answers to our cries: "Yes," "No," and "Wait, my child."

This journey of mine and my husband's is an ongoing one that will continue until we meet Him face to face. We are two imperfect people with baggage and stubborn wills. It is messy at times, but God is using our journey to be a beacon to others as they follow a similar path. If we refocus our eyes on Him and listen to what He is speaking to our hearts, we will complete this journey together and be the witnesses He is calling us to be.

We are all on a journey. I am not anyone special. I am, again, one beggar showing another one where to find food. He is our sustenance. He will meet you in your pain too. This is just one of my Holy Echoes stories where He met me when I needed Him most. He will meet you there too. Call on Him.

Listen...

When I finally slowed down from the whirlwind of work and the weekends away, I started to listen again. I was given three separate scriptures that started to repeat—slowly at first, and then before I even realized it, I was posting and hearing them everywhere. These verses were in order, and over the months I noticed them getting louder.

My first verse... listen

Luke 10:41-42

"'Martha, Martha,' the Lord answered, 'you are worried and upset about many things, but few things are needed—or indeed only one. Mary has chosen what is better, and it will not be taken away from her.'"

In my haste to get things done, I am often like Martha in the Bible. She was rushing around and worrying about what needed to be done for the day, the week, and the month. I am Martha personified. I have a goal. I get out my spreadsheets and yellow highlighter to create the plan of attack. Then, piece by piece, I implement the plan, and from there I capture each step like a chess player until I have captured the queen. I am driven to make the plan successful. No matter what happens, I strive to hit that goal. Often, in my haste, I leave bodies in the wake. I push so hard to meet the goal and ring the bell, so to speak, that others are hurt in the process. I crave order deep in my soul, and if I can do anything to accomplish this order, I run with great zeal until it is captured, like a lion racing after its prey.

I am not like Mary. I have a ridiculously hard time sitting and listening to the Lord. It kills me to sit for any length of time to do anything. Planes, lines, traffic. I perceive them as the enemies of my life. The thought of sitting for any length of time without doing something is as foreign to me as learning a new language from a faraway country... blindfolded. It is like ants climbing up my leg at a picnic. I want to jump up and start swiping them away and remove myself from the spot in the shade. The enemy uses those moments when I am pressing in and praying to sling darts of guilt at my mind. *I have so much to do. How can I stop and rest? Others are working hard, and I am just sitting here. I can do this later and just get back on track with my chores.* So many words of guilt.

When I stop to think about these words of guilt, I realize they are old tapes from my past. I wasn't good enough unless I was accomplishing something. Again, the enemy uses old tapes and lies to distort and distract from His truth. The truth is that I need to silence the noise around me. The noise of the world can be distracting and can push me farther from His voice. "Come and sit with Me," He calls quietly. He does speak in the storm of our lives. But often we are so busy, we can't hear His voice softly saying, "Come and step away for a moment. I have so much to share with you." He longs for our conversation, like an old friend waiting for the phone to ring. The remarkable thing is that God is faster than the phone, a Zoom call, or even sound. Think about that. How awesome is God, that He is here to speak to us without a formal meeting request? The Creator of the universe is on speed dial. We only need to step aside and listen quietly.

Time is short. Life is short. Take time and pull up a chair to His table, to hear Him speak to you. You won't regret the moments alone in His presence.

What I also learned from meditating on these verses is that God is not calling me to become a Mary. I am a Martha. He created me as a Martha, to get things done. However, He is calling me to step aside and focus on Him each day, to bring out the Mary inside of me. This time alone with Him is giving me refreshment and renewal of my spirit, like an ice-cold drink on a hot day. I cannot go non-stop without taking breaks for refueling my soul. We cannot pour into others from an empty cup. I am not effective if I am drained and spent from "doing" non-stop. I need to stop and bring out the Mary within me. Afterward, I can then rise up as the Martha He created and conquer my lists with His help. Thank you, Lord. Are you a Mary or a Martha? Ask God to reveal today how He can use your gifts.

Ready Yourselves...

My second verse... get ready

Luke 10:2-3

"He told them, 'The harvest is plentiful, but the workers are few. Ask the Lord of the harvest, therefore, to send out workers into his harvest field. Go! I am sending you out like lambs among wolves.'"

"Get ready." These were interesting words to be given. I was told to get ready before 2020. I had grand ideas in my head of what God was getting us ready to do as a couple. How funny is that—in my small mind, I had *no* idea He was calling me to get ready for 2020. This time, when He spoke the words, He added another one: "Again." "Get ready again." Whew... for what, Lord? For the harvest.

Throughout the past year I have been using the scripture, "The harvest is plenty, but the workers are few." I used this reference for our company. We were blessed by an abundance of work. And by blessed, I mean overwhelmingly blessed—to the point of overflowing, spilling out of our cup. Thank you, Lord! But we needed people! We couldn't hire a warm body for this abundance of work. *The workers are few, Lord. Help!* The process of seeking employees in our own strength began. As you laugh a bit at that statement, remember we all do it... After a long road of struggles, my husband and I have handed it over to the Great Employer who can find us the right people. After pushing

175

against the "pull" door for a year, we decided to do it His way. He was saying, "Not yet; wait." Love those words... well, not really, but learning to love them. This was also a revelation of what He is going through. He needs willing workers for His harvest. How patient is our God...

So, back to my story. "Get ready again" was spoken into my spirit. The workers are few. There is a spiritual awakening occurring through 2020 and beyond. I have said over and over that 2020 was the greatest time to share the love of God. The workers are few. He needs us to reach those searching for Him. The workers are few. Do you hear the drumbeat getting closer? Our time is short. Read Revelation. He is speaking to His people to stand up and start sharing their story. It is time to share your story. Plant seeds and reap the harvest.

He will bring the people to us. We need to be open to His Spirit and share our testimony. My testimony is here. I need to complete this and start sharing more with everyone. He will do the rest. It is now your turn. Step in and share your story.

...For Such a Time as This

My third verses... speak what I am sharing

Esther 4:14-16

"For if you remain silent at this time, relief and deliverance for the Jews will arise from another place, but you and your father's family will perish. And who knows but that you have come to your royal position for such a time as this?"

"Then Esther sent this reply to Mordecai: 'Go, gather together all the Jews who are in Susa, and fast for me. Do not eat or drink for three days, night or day. I and my attendants will fast as you do. When this is done, I will go to the king, even though it is against the law. And if I perish, I perish.'"

Isn't it funny how God often uses the foolish to give wisdom to the wise? I am one of His chief fools. I make mistakes daily and often do what *I* want instead of what He is calling me to do. I find myself daily on my knees, asking for grace and mercy as I messed up once again. How can God use such a fool like me? I ask that question over and over. With my tattered past and shaky footing on my future, I question His role in my life. Have you ever felt the same way?

There have been many people of the Bible who felt the same. Moses, who couldn't speak. Esther, who felt unqualified. Even Jonah, who outright refused because of fear of where he was led.

When I accepted Christ into my life many years ago, He began to speak to me. I was blessed by the transforming words of peace and focus. Then He began to ask me to share what I heard and saw. I asked, "Why, Lord? These words are for me. How am I supposed to share them with others?" As the Spirit spoke to me the words to share with others, I held back in fear. "Who am I to say anything? I am nobody. I am not educated in this field. That is why You have called pastors to the ministry, Lord, not me." He quietly encouraged me. I stifled the Spirit and held back. Again, I am the chief of fools. However, like a loving Father, He kept speaking to my heart. When I took the time to sit like Mary, He would pour into my soul His words of love and encouragement. Then He would whisper into my heart to share what I saw and heard.

This was a struggle. I wish I could say that it ended quickly; however, it took years. God is patient and will not push His will on us. We need to come to Him willingly and listen and act. He can bring us to the moment of realization. The stipulation is that He gave us free will to act. He is gracious and encourages us along the way, like a parent guiding a wayward child.

I woke up one morning right before the alarm and heard, *"Wake up."* "Okay, Lord, I am awake, what are you telling me?" Then the alarm went off. "Wake *up*; time is short." I went to my Bible and started searching. Jeremiah 49:14 resonated with me. *"I have heard a message from the Lord; an envoy was sent to the nations to say, 'Assemble yourselves to attack it! Rise up for battle!'"*

What a weird scripture, I thought to myself. This was a battle cry to action. If anyone knows me well, I am not a morning person—and action, when it occurs, is after coffee and a minute or two. "Wake *up,*" I kept hearing. "Okay, Lord, I am awake." Who needs to hear this besides me?

I walked into the conference room with my husband and kept hearing the slow beat of the drum... "Wake up." I brought our speaker and felt led to play "Rise Up" by Cain. As it played, I felt refreshed as the words reached the couples walking in for the morning. I walked around the room and asked how to share it. I proceeded to the pastor in the room and quietly shared with him. He understood. During his message later, he requested that I share the verse. It was supposed to be a part of the message He was sharing with all in the room. We were being called to battle for marriages with the Lord. This was a battle cry.

If I had not shared this message, God would have found another way to do so. But I stepped out in faith and shared it. He took all the glory, and I received confirmation to keep stepping out in faith. Even as imperfect as I am. He shared with me that others will hear and listen.

Here is a word for us today. Sitting on the plane heading home, listening to music, He called me in. I felt the Holy Spirit descend on the plane in the air and felt Him calling me to come closer. "Be still, read my words, and share with everyone." I felt surrounded by the Spirit. The love and clarity of mind was so intense.

Jeremiah speaks for God in His book. He speaks throughout Jeremiah of repentance and restoration to a wayward Israel. "Repent, and come back to your first love." Like a small flame in the bottom of an altar, flickering, the words settled into my spirit. This book was written thousands of years ago. However, He was calling *us*. He is our first love. We need to come back to Him. He is calling us to repent and dig deeper. We need to get our house in order and get ready. The drumbeat is getting louder. We don't have as much time as we believe. It is time to come back to our first love. He is calling. He is waiting. Will you join me?

Joel 2:28

"And afterward, I will pour out my Spirit on all people. Your sons and daughters will prophesy, your old men will dream dreams, your young men will see visions."

Building and Rebuilding Walls

The year 2020 taught me many lessons. One of the lessons we learned was to make updating our home a priority. So many things got in the way of our projects at home. Mainly the business, and not having enough time either at the end of the day or on weekends. Both of us are so tired by the day's end that we just want to sit and "veg" on the couch and not plan another project. We had worked on some of the rooms in the house over the years but lost steam as life took over. After spending months fixing up and selling my little home we had rented to the kids, we both decided it was time to start working on our home again. It was time for a new season of change.

We spend a fair amount of time at the end of the day sitting on the couch, sharing stories or watching reruns of old shows we love. Staring back at us is our fireplace mantel that has been "in progress" for many years. The mantel, if you can call it one, was basically a painted form around the fireplace. My husband re-did the drywall around the fireplace to make it more uniform years ago. We were going to place stone on the fireplace and add an actual mantel, but again, time was not on our side. We had even purchased a piece of stone as a sample of what we wanted to use. So, we stared at the painted frame around the fireplace, with the one lonely piece of stone propped up, year after year.

This particular year, after Christmas, we decided that it was time to start tackling the mantel. All of our home projects are seen through a viewpoint of someday selling the house. We want it done perfectly for the next owners. So, first we went online, looking for a mantel. We found one that seemed to fit the fireplace and the room perfectly. However, the size and weight were daunting, and I was concerned about whether it would make it to our home in one piece. We ordered the mantel and then began the process of finding stone.

I had wanted to take the one piece of stone we'd had collecting dust on our mantel for many years to the store as an example of color and shape. However, I remembered the stone after we had arrived at the store. It was sitting at home. We walked through the entire store and came upon a section that caught our interest. After much discussion, we picked out the stone we wanted and placed the order. When the stone arrived at our home, I picked one up and brought it to the fireplace. The lonely stone that had been sitting there for years was its missing twin. We had picked the same pattern. That was a confirmation.

The next four weeks transformed our living room into a construction site as we brought in the scaffolding and all the materials to attach the stone to the fireplace. The mantel arrived and was more massive than I had originally thought. I wondered how we would get it into the house. My husband, the creative one, had a lift for our business. This lift was as massive as the mantel. I helped him as he placed the lift in front of the fireplace and attached gas piping to help bring the mantel closer to the fireplace. He then secured the mantel professionally, as if he did it every day. I am constantly amazed at the talent that man has.

The process of placing the stone on the mantel was no small feat, either. Using the scaffolding and working as a team, we accomplished the project. Carl would mix the "glue" for the wall and quickly paint the wall with it, and I would hand him each section of stone to attach. Each step seemed to take so long, but after time, we would see our progress and press on. One very long weekend later, we completed the wall. We then put a protective coating on the stone and the mantel. When we added the coating, the colors of the stone and mantel came to life. It took on a whole new look, and the multi-colored stone had new dimension. Carl then added a track light above the fireplace to shine light on the wall. I stepped back and was so impressed by the work we had done as a team. It was breathtaking.

As the last part of the coating was completed, I felt the Lord tugging at my heart. This was not just a fireplace. It was a wall of protection. It was to be a reminder that He was hedging us in daily. After completing the fireplace, we took some oil and dedicated it to Him. He is our protection, but the wall was our reminder. Every night as we sit on our couch together, I look up at the fireplace and remember His promises. How awesome is our God to remind us of His love in the projects we complete? What projects are you working on that God can use? Pray for His wisdom as you work on that project. He will meet you there.

Job 1:10

"Have you not put a hedge around him and his household and everything he has? You have blessed the work of his hands, so that his flocks and herds are spread throughout the land."

Psalm 125:2

"As the mountains surround Jerusalem, so

the Lord surrounds his people both now and forevermore."

Philippians 4:6

"Do not be anxious about anything, but in every situation, by prayer and petition, with thanksgiving, present your requests to God."

Going Higher

Every time I come closer to my heavenly Father by reading scripture or praising through music, I am amazed at how He meets me there. It is not always the same each time. Sometimes I am given the peace that passes all understanding, knowing He is with me. Other times I am given a word, or a direction. Sometimes, honestly, I "feel" nothing. It doesn't mean that He isn't there with me. I might be under the weather, or there may be something else capturing my thoughts or feelings. Feelings should not be the barometer of who He is or how close we are to Him. As a young believer, I used to believe that the more I "felt" His presence, the closer I was to Him. It took a while to realize that was not true. God does not leave us. Even when we don't "feel" it. He is always there. His love is always firm. Someone once told me that God is always "live streaming." We can reach out to Him any time of the day or night, and He is there. How cool is that?

There are seasons where God has allowed me to go through a valley and not "feel" his presence. Those times He is stretching and growing me and my faith. The stretching is like a rubber band being pulled into two directions simultaneously. When you stretch a rubber band, you are also keeping it from becoming brittle.

I had a drawer full of rubber bands that my mother had saved for years. Mom collected and saved a lot of office supplies. I put them together and called it my "Mom drawer." I was excited to have these on hand, so whenever I needed them, I could reach in the drawer and put one to use. One day I reached into the famous "Mom drawer" to grab a rubber band and discovered something new. The rubber bands had not been used in years, so they were brittle, and when I tried to wrap one around my notes, the rubber band immediately broke. We feel the stretch and "feel" alone. However, our heavenly Father is with us, and uses the stretching period to keep us from becoming brittle and to learn a lesson. I can't say that I like the stretching part, because like an infant who wants to be held constantly, I want to "feel" God's closeness daily.

I rejoice when I am in a season where I feel His presence. It is like a perfect sunny day with no clouds in sight. God uses those moments to speak love and words into my heart so I can follow His next direction for me. I cling to the memories of those times when I am not "feeling" His love. God is so faithful that during those close times, He uses others to confirm what I've heard.

One flight home with my husband, God used that quiet moment to speak to me. I was feeling exhausted and wanted to just close my eyes and relive the amazing trip we'd had, visiting one of our kids and our newest grandbaby. My husband rested quietly next to me, and I turned on my music and closed my eyes. "Open your Bible app," I heard. I opened my eyes and reached for my phone. I opened the Bible app and started to read. I felt the weariness of my body take over and closed the app. "Open the Bible app," I heard again. So, once again I picked up the phone and asked where I was supposed to read. I started where I had left off in one chapter, and then felt led to 1 Corinthians 2. As I read the chapter, my eyes became focused on three specific verses, three through five.

I highlighted the verses and asked what He wanted me to

learn from them. As I reread the verses, I heard Him relate how I am the one who is weak and unschooled, but through the Holy Spirit's power, I could share His words. I felt humbled and grateful for the valuable lesson. As I sat and meditated on His words for me, I heard another direction. "Copy these verses and send them out to a pastor and his wife." I have felt led to send out verses before, but this time it was very late at night, and who was I to send them a message? I wasn't sure of the direction and sat on it for a minute. Finally, after contemplating a Jonah moment, I quickly copied the verses and sent out the message. The interesting part of this moment is that the recipient of the message would not receive it until I landed, because my phone was in airplane mode. I prayed it wouldn't disturb their night and be heard, not by me, but by God. I closed my phone and my eyes for the rest of the trip. We arrived safely back to our home airport, and due to my weariness, I forgot about the event and drove home.

The next morning, I opened my phone to a text from the pastor and his wife. They praised God for my message, because they had been praying and worshiping that night for an hour, seeking God's will for events that were coming up. Those specific verses were an answer from God. They thanked me for my willingness to share what God wanted them to hear. I could not have known what was happening across the country in their living room. I felt so humbled to be a vessel for His words. I also felt the confirmation that I was doing what He asked, and it wasn't in my own strength. If I hadn't been obedient, we would all have missed the blessing. You never know when or where He is going to use you. Step out in faith today when you hear His voice.

Psalm 139:8

"If I go up to the heavens, you are there; if I make my bed in the depths, you are there."

1 Corinthians 2:3-5

"I came to you in weakness with great fear and trembling. My message and my preaching were not with wise and persuasive words, but with a demonstration of the Spirit's power, so that your faith might not rest on human wisdom, but on God's power."

I Am Still Praying, Lord

Have you ever made plans and then felt confident that God was amused by the goals? I have spent many years making plans and then watching them fail or turn in a different direction that I never saw coming. When I was much younger, I had a plan for my life. I didn't have a personal relationship with God but knew He was there somewhere. I judged that nothing was going to happen in my life unless I stepped in and made it happen. As a teenager, my plans were to move to New York City and become an interior designer living in a high rise, alone. I was like a blind person trying to tackle driving. I am glad God didn't allow those plans to succeed. I do feel confident now that God was probably shaking His head as a Father does, and then gently steering me back on course to Him and His plans.

The moment when I realized that His plans were better than my own, I started praying for guidance and wisdom. These prayers became more passionate as the mountains in front of me grew bigger. I wanted to follow His blueprint for me, but often I became scared by the enormity of the goal or obstacle in the way. I am sure that is one of the reasons why He doesn't share the end story with us. Keeping close to my heavenly Father through prayer helps strengthen me as I follow His direction for my life. My prayer life has evolved from basic requests to cries and groans sometimes, as my relationship with God expands. As we get closer to our heavenly Father, we learn we can come to Him for everything, and pretenses are not needed. He is an all-knowing God who knows our thoughts before we speak them out loud. We don't need to hide behind fancy words or phrases. I am so grateful for that.

My husband and I watched as God blessed our business when I came home to assist. He grew the business monthly as we pressed closer to Him, asking for guidance and wisdom. We thought it couldn't get any better as He brought the customers and work to us. Then we hit a roadblock. We had so much work that we needed more employees. When I came home to work in the office, I honestly didn't think I would need office assistance. My husband knew and shared that with me the day I started in the business. I believed his view was a bit of an overreach. Two years into the business, I had to apologize to my husband because he was right, and I had underestimated God again.

We started to pray for wisdom and discernment as we placed advertisements for new technicians. Again, as I tried to interpret God's plan, I assumed He wanted us to have several employees to cover the work that was increasing daily. My husband and I became disillusioned as the months passed with no bites for the position. The few we did receive were blatantly unqualified. I pressed harder and prayed harder. I thought maybe I wasn't praying the right prayer. I started to second-guess myself. Why would God bring us the work and not the help? What was I missing? My husband and I shared our frustrations with each other and with God. I must have been so consumed by the task at hand that I missed the message, and He gave it to Carl. My husband stated one day that God had told him we were slowing down for a reason. The momentum of the business was going to take a break, because other responsibilities were coming. My first inclination was to worry, because I didn't want to lose all that we had worked for. Then, after a time of prayer, I realized that He had not brought us this far to fail. He had other plans for us, and we couldn't do them all at once. He knows the beginning from the end, remember? How often do we forget that statement and run out in our own strength? We miss the quiet message in the process. I am thankful for my husband, who heard the quiet message while I scurried about like a squirrel collecting nuts for the winter. Do you feel harried today? Reach out to a knowing God, who can still the waters within you.

Proverbs 16:9

"In their hearts humans plan their course, but the Lord establishes their steps."

Romans 8:26

"In the same way, the Spirit helps us in our weakness. We do not know what we ought to pray for, but the Spirit himself intercedes for us through wordless groans."

Steps of Faith

As our business grew, space to hold the equipment for jobs became an issue. We only have so much room. Equipment began to take over our garage, our basement, and the trailer that was purchased to hold the tractor. There was no room for anything. My car sat outside the garage, pouting. Or was that me? I think it was me. Either way, you couldn't walk anywhere in our home without seeing skids and boxes taking over the scenery.

We purchase equipment ahead of time when a job is secured for two reasons. One, to be fiscally responsible as a business. For those who are not familiar with accounting, I will not bore you with the lengthy details. Suffice it to say, having the equipment purchased ahead of the job avoids placing the deposit in a separate account. The second reason we purchase equipment ahead of the job is to avoid any issues with finding parts or equipment. After COVID there has been a massive shortage of specific equipment and parts. Also, the cost of most equipment or supplies has increased drastically due to the shortage. Manufacturers are dealing with materials and employee shortages. These shortages trickle down to small businesses like ours.

We decided that we needed a shed to store the equipment and the tractor we used for work. In December of 2020, my husband and I started to look at sheds. After reviewing the size needed, we decided to look at pole barns. The size and scope of the project grew as we discussed the need. I had thoughts of a small pole barn to hold equipment. My husband Carl had other ideas. After sitting with a local builder, I saw the small pole barn increase into a size that completely overwhelmed me. As I may have mentioned before, when we plan any project for the house or our property, we do so in the light of selling to a future owner. I believed that a pole barn would be useful for said future owner. I just didn't think it needed to hold their small airplane.

I knew that God was asking us to build the barn in faith. I also knew that He wasn't sending us any new employees with all the work we were receiving. It seemed like a major contradiction to me. My husband felt confident that God was calling us to build this barn. I prayed and in faith, agreed. The process of completion was another challenge. The builder had material shortages and weather issues and was attempting to build several barns at the same time. The project was supposed to take two to three weeks once started. This original schedule would accommodate the multitude of large boxes that came daily. However, the project ended up taking four months to complete.

Patience and prayer got me through those four months. Many frustrated calls and schedule changes later, we finally saw the results. I have to say, it was akin to watching paint dry. Remember how patient I am? The builder asked what I wanted on the cupola. I chose the eagle, because the barn would be His and Isaiah 40:31 was given to me. I am working on a plaque to attach over the garage door as a reminder that He will renew our strength daily.

This is where you would expect that I would share why God asked us to build the barn so large. I don't have the answer yet. Do we always have the answer to the question right away? Sometimes God says, "Just trust Me and step out in faith." We are still in the process of stepping out in faith, knowing He is in control of our business, our finances, and our lives. Who better to give everything to than an all-knowing God? He knows the beginning from the end. He has plans for our "little shed," as Carl calls it. I can't wait to see what His plans will be. Remember, you don't always need to know the why—only to obey. What is He asking you to build today?

Galatians 5:25

"Since we live by the Spirit, let us keep in step with the Spirit."

Isaiah 40:31

"But those who hope in the Lord will renew their strength. They will soar on wings like eagles; they will run and not grow weary, they will walk and not be faint."

Loving Enough to Let Go

I have learned a lot of lessons over the years of walking with God. One of the harder lessons is being a mom and letting go of an adult child into God's hands. It is so easy being a parent when your kids are young. I hear young mothers yelling at me right now. "That is *not* true!" Hang on. Give me a minute, and I will explain why. When you have a newborn, I agree that you are faced with a multitude of challenges. Eating and sleep schedules are the hardest at first.

I am not a morning person, and honestly, I am not a happy person if I don't get enough sleep. Having a newborn challenges your sleep patterns, and you learn quickly to nap whenever and wherever you can. Knowing why a baby cries is an art of its own. Are they wet? Are they in pain? Are they hungry? We often learn that sometimes there are no answers, and we just hold them closely and pray as they strengthen their tiny lungs. One of my children had colic, and I spent every night for months walking him back and forth in our apartment for hours, holding him close to my chest for warmth as he cried. It nearly broke my heart. I thought I was the worst parent. Somehow you get through the early stages, attempting to keep a sense of humor, and pray it gets easier as they get older. I kept saying to myself, "At least I can dress them the way I want."

Then comes the crawling and walking stage. Fear again takes over, and you wonder how you had so many dangerous items in your house, and no one died. Another child of mine seemed to have a magnet on his head which was attracted to every sharp corner he went near. We ended up in the emergency room three times before he was two. Once again, I felt like a horrible parent. But wait—the pre-teen years are right around the corner. I kept the same sense of humor, looking for the bright side. "At least I can tell them what to do."

Raising a pre-teen takes a new level of patience and prayer. I sharpened my prayer life in raising my three. I felt called to bring them home to homeschool for a season. One child was reading on her own, way above her grade level. She needed encouragement and space to move forward faster. The second child needed space to be himself without distracting others. He was the "entertainment committee" and got along with anyone who met him. Our third child was a reminder that I was human and would not make it without God's help and divine interference. As each child went into their teen years, I became more aware of how much I didn't know. Every time I thought I had the parenting thing figured out, another situation would arise and remind me of how much I needed my heavenly Father to help me through it all. I also kept my sense of humor, most days. "At least I can share some wisdom before they eat me out of house and home."

Then they become adults. We work so hard to get them to this point that we forget there are going to be more challenges. The first time I watched one of my kids leave the house to move out on his own, my heart broke. How was I going to fix anything if I wasn't there? Had I taught them enough to face the big world they were going to join? I struggled with guilt because I was a young, naïve mother who grew spiritually as I taught what I could to my children before they left home. I didn't have all the answers, and I wasn't sure I even gave the right ones before they left.

All I could do was pray for their adult journey. I couldn't dress them. I couldn't tell them where they could go. Sometimes I couldn't even share wisdom, because they believed their way was now better. They had to learn all the hard lessons I learned growing up. I wish we could fast-forward and help them learn without all the pain involved. When I remarried, my husband brought four more kids to the equation. There were so many moving parts. We became a blended family and the challenges and prayers continued. This also opened my heart to love each of my "new kids" just as much as I loved my three. I wanted the best for *all* our kids. I was reminded that we all belong to God. He accepts us as openly as He accepted His chosen people, the Israelites. How cool is it that He showed me this through this process?

I pray for each of our seven children to have a deep relationship with our heavenly Father, because I know that will help them through all their challenges in life. Watching your adult children struggle with their own faith walk is hard as a parent as well. I love our seven children so much that I would take a bullet for them. I constantly tell them that there is nothing they could do which would make me stop loving them. That is how a parent is. That is also how our heavenly Father is with us. He often shares these thoughts with me when I become frustrated with one of our kids. How patient has He been with me? I have strayed, ignored, or pushed back His guidance, believing that I knew better. He patiently works in me daily as I learn that His process is better than mine. As I place my children in His loving hands, I pray He gives them His wisdom and discernment in their life's journey. Pray for your family today. You never know where God will lead that prayer.

Proverbs 22:6

"Start children off on the way they should go, and even when they are old they will not turn from it."

Proverbs 3:5 (NIV)

"Trust in the Lord with all your heart and lean not on your own understanding."

The Perfect Storm

Sometimes the lessons we learn are from simple yet humorous events in our lives. This story is one of many that God has used to give me perspective and humor at the same time.

One Christmas many years ago, my husband decided that we needed a robot vacuum cleaner. For those who do not know what that is, a robot vacuum is a round disc approximately twelve inches in diameter that has several sweeping brushes to pick up debris, and a pocket that holds the dust bunnies until opened and cleaned out. The robot is automated through a cell phone by an app and can go all through the house without falling downstairs. I have to say, the ability to not fall down the stairs impressed me the most. It has sensors that realize there is no more space underneath it and just turns around. This app on your phone can also set the time and days you want to vacuum. When I first heard about the robot vacuum, I have to say I was a bit skeptical. How could a robot clean as well as our current vacuum?

Skepticism aside, I must admit that our tiny mechanical creature is pretty awesome. It picks up dirt and debris in between our regular vacuum schedules like crazy. It is a tiny household helper that doesn't complain and just does its business every day while we conquer our workday activities. After setting up our robot, I became used to my miniature maid as it started its day every morning at 10 a.m.

It would dutifully make a chime announcing its day was beginning and then proceed to go all around the house without complaint for an hour. After the hour was up, the robot would proceed to go back to its docking station to charge until the next day. The puppies got used to its interference as well. Sometimes the robot would get stuck under a piece of furniture, and both puppies would run and let me know so I could save it from perceived possible harm and send it back on its journey. I was so proud of my husband's decision to purchase the robot and told everyone we knew.

Everything was going great for a couple years, until one afternoon. I was training a new employee at our home office, and the puppies were unusually quiet as the robot did its thing. I suddenly realized that the robot was not making its rounds and wondered if they had forgotten to let me know what happened. It was not like them to let it get stuck without notifying me. I walked into the kitchen and realized why they had not spoken up.

One of the dogs had had stomach distress, and instead of letting me know, he had chosen to go on the kitchen floor. The dutiful robot vacuum had headed straight for the mess the dog had left behind and had proceeded to "clean" it up. My kitchen floor looked like a murder scene, but not with blood. However, not only was my kitchen tainted, but so were the rest of the areas the robot had decided to travel until it got stuck. The puppies looked at me with a combination of disbelief and guilt.

I immediately grabbed the robot and turned it off. I then started the process of disinfecting my entire house. Afterward, I went back to the robot and turned it over. The enormity of the mess underneath was beyond my comprehension—and honestly, I contemplated throwing the entire thing away. Instead, I left it in time out, away from everyone, until my husband came home.

Side note: my husband is the hero of this story. He spent one afternoon cleaning and disinfecting the robot until it was ready to conquer another day. We still have the robot, and few close friends were told about the messy story, until today.

The lesson I learned was not to trust fully in the vacuum, or unattended puppies. I trusted in what I knew and not what could happen. I assumed that I knew everything the robot could do, and proudly admitted often how great the robot was and how smart we were to purchase it. My lessons that day were in pride and a moment of humility. It was a proverbial "poop show," but a lesson I won't ever forget. The messy lessons can often be the best ones that we never forget. Do you have a story like this? Remember, God uses all stories to teach us and those around us.

Proverbs 11:2

"When pride comes, then comes disgrace, but with humility comes wisdom."

Proverbs 28:26

"Those who trust in themselves are fools, but those who walk in wisdom are kept safe."

The End of the Trail, or Just the Beginning?

This last story was written for you. This isn't the end of our journey together. It is, in fact, just the beginning. God willing, I will continue down this path to share more Holy Echoes as He gives me stories. But what about you? If some of my stories have shown you a moment in time where you also saw God speak to you, then I judge that I have succeeded. Each time we get closer to Him, we can hear His still, small voice, sharing His deepest thoughts and love for you. I am an ordinary person who just put down on paper what He has shared with me over the years. What is He sharing with you today? Take time to step aside and be still and listen.

God spoke words to my heart as I was completing this book. The words are: "It is later than you think." You might judge that you have a lot of time left here on this small blue planet. But none of us knows when our time will come. My husband and I went away for an event recently, and when we came back home, our grandfather clock was silent. It was eerily quiet when we walked through the door. We weren't greeted by the familiar chimes of the day. The clock had stopped at 2:30. I had thought we had time left before the chains on the clock needed to be wound back up. I had misjudged the clock, and I ran out of time. Again, none of us know when our time will come. He wants us to take stock in our lives today and every day we are here.

How can we do this? First, He wants us to renew and come

back to our first love. Have you become lukewarm or cold? Turn around today if you have steered away from Him. It only takes one step. Turn and walk back to Him, where He has been waiting for you. If you don't know Him personally and want to know more, reach out to someone who can share the Bible with you. They will share His love story with you. Read John 3:16-17,

"For God so loved the world that he gave his one and only Son, that whoever believes in him shall not perish but have eternal life. For God did not send his Son into the world to condemn the world, but to save the world through him."

He has been waiting for you all your life. Don't turn away while you are so close.

Next, He wants us to refresh by digging deeper and learning more about Him. Refresh by opening your Bible and reading His love story to you. He will meet you there when you seek Him. Meditate on His Word, and you will rediscover new joy as you read each book of the Bible. He says in Jeremiah 33:3,

"Call to me and I will answer you and tell you great and unsearchable things you do not know."

How awesome is God that He has new things to share with us daily? All we have to do is lean in and seek His face.

Finally, He is calling us to engage by getting ready for the harvest and His coming. Listen for the chimes. Time is running out. Step out of your comfort zone and join the harvest. Share your testimony today to bring someone closer to Him. One small pebble in the water can form multiple rings. You can be a part of the next great revival. God willing, we will meet here again for more Holy Echoes. Keep looking for Him in the everyday events of your life.

Revelation 22:20

"He who testifies to these things says, 'Yes, I am coming soon.' Amen. Come, Lord Jesus."

Matthew 9:37

"Then he said to his disciples, 'The harvest is plentiful but the workers are few.'"

Matthew 24:36-41

"But about that day or hour no one knows, not even the angels in heaven, nor the Son, but only the Father. As it was in the days of Noah, so it will be at the coming of the Son of Man. For in the days before the flood, people were eating and drinking, marrying and giving in marriage, up to the day Noah entered the ark; and they knew nothing about what would happen until the flood came and took them all away. That is how it will be at the coming of the Son of Man. Two men will be in the field; one will be taken and the other left. Two women will be grinding with a hand mill; one will be taken and the other left."

References

United Marriage Encounter. https://unitedmarriage.com/

For King & Country, for KING & COUNTRY. https://www.forkingandcountry.com/

Kintsugi. https://en.wikipedia.org/wiki/Kintsugi

Crowder. https://www.crowdermusic.com/

Cain. https://www.caintheband.com/

John Sherrill, Elizabeth Sherrill, Corrie ten Boom, *The Hiding Place: The Triumphant True Story of Corrie Ten Boom* (Bantam Books, 1974).

Beth Moore, *Praying God's Word* (B&H Publishing Group, 2009).

CPSIA information can be obtained
at www.ICGtesting.com
Printed in the USA
FSHW021331141021
85391FS